Praise for *Hard-Won Wisdom*

"Jathan Janove's title of his new book 'Hard-Won Wisdom' is spot-on for the priceless wisdom he sets forth throughout every chapter in this book. I wish I had this 'wisdom' when I started my career 38 years ago! Rather than looking at human resources issues in the traditional legal way, we learn to look at these issues before they start in a humanistic manner so as to prevent the issues in the first place—what a concept!"

—Charles Castner, Labor & Employment corporate counsel,
Daimler Trucks North America LLC

"Every manager has the ability and the opportunity to step up his or her game, and Jathan Janove's book will help you do so. With a series of interesting vignettes, lifted from his many years of experience as a labor lawyer and consultant, Janove draws the reader in. Each vignette ends with a crisp summary of the moral of his story, resulting in a wealth of useful advice and guidance, and making learning easy."

—Susan Meisinger, columnist for *HRExecutive Online* and former President &
CEO of the Society for Human Resource Management (SHRM)

"Wow, I truly wish I had this book as a leadership manual when I started my senior management position. It is written like I am sitting with Jathan and over a cup of coffee discussing personnel and leadership issues. The book is a guidebook, a textbook, and an engaging read that would sit on the corner of my desk."

—Ken Couch, R.Ph., retired president of Smith Drug Company
and president of J M Smith Corporation

"We really value our employees at Ventas and want to make sure they know it. We also want to effectively assess, coach and develop our employees to bring out the best in them and create high functioning teams. Jathan's vignettes and practical advice provide clear and easy ways to improve our day to day interactions with employees and re-frame our approach on key issues in the workplace."

—Debra A. Cafaro, Chairman & CEO, Ventas, Inc. (NYSE: VTR)

"Every human resources professional knows that how an organization responds to workplace behaviors can make or break a company. This is a must read for anyone looking to improve employee engagement and drive higher levels of performance within their organization. Jathan's highly entertaining stories offer practical advice that helps you navigate the many landmines that exist in the workplace today."

—Tracy Stachniak, director of Human Resources and
Training & Development, Toyota Material Handling, U.S.A. Inc.

"As one who has experienced the benefits of Jathan's wisdom throughout my organization for over 15 years, let me say that HARD-WON WISDOM walks the talk. From Star Profiles, to Same Day Summaries, Jathan's practical approach, combined with Zen-like, out-of-the-box coaching, strengthens companies, people, relationships, and team building. Simply said, we are a better company, with better people, creating better results for our stakeholders because of his shared wisdom. Jathan is a testament to 'real communication' in the workplace, and HARD-WON WISDOM is an enjoyable read providing insight gained through decades of research, observation, experience, and trial. The stories will make you laugh, while at the same time, creating a number of 'aha' moments for anyone who is responsible for managing people and teams."

—Danuel Stanger, chief asset officer,
Bridge Investment Group Holdings, LLC

"Jathan Janove understands the intersection of engagement, accountability, leadership and results in the workplace. He appreciates the business of the workplace, the need for fun, and how to keep those intact while doing the right thing. Through good storytelling that is an enjoyable read, the book provides managers with practical methods to accomplish good leadership. Whether you are managing a large multinational organization, a small start-up, or a family, everyone can benefit from the Jathan's book."

—Charlotte L. Miller, chief human resources officer,
U.S. Ski and Snowboard Association

"I was pleased to see the word "Wisdom" in Jathan's book title. In the many roles Jathan has played for our company, his wisdom has positively impacted several decisions we've made over the years. Jathan's management principles have embedded themselves as a core element in our company's culture. His employment law counsel and his management training courses have effectively helped to shape 1-800 Contacts into a great work environment. If one observed the coaching sessions within our walls, Jathan's terminology, such as "same day summary", "star profile" and "EAR method" will commonly be heard. True-to-form Jathan's book shares the compelling stories and management advice that we have come to rely on in an easy-to-read and enjoyable format. A must-read for anyone currently in, or aspiring to be in a management role."

—Rod Lacey, chief people officer, 1-800 CONTACTS, Inc.

"I'm in a unique position to comment on Jathan's book since he reported to me when serving as managing shareholder of our Portland and Seattle offices. I can tell you first-hand that his stuff works—even on me!"

—Charles B. Baldwin, managing director, Ogletree,
Deakins, Nash, Smoak & Stewart, P.C.

HARD-WON WISDOM

TRUE STORIES FROM THE MANAGEMENT TRENCHES

JATHAN JANOVE

AMACOM

AMERICAN MANAGEMENT ASSOCIATION

New York • Atlanta • Brussels • Chicago • Mexico City • San Francisco
Shanghai • Tokyo • Toronto • Washington, D. C.

Bulk discounts available. For details visit:
www.amacombooks.org/go/specialsales
Or contact special sales:
Phone: 800-250-5308
Email: specialsls@amanet.org
View all the AMACOM titles at: www.amacombooks.org
American Management Association: www.amanet.org

This publication is designed to provide accurate and authoritative information in regard to the subject matter covered. It is sold with the understanding that the publisher is not engaged in rendering legal, accounting, or other professional service. If legal advice or other expert assistance is required, the services of a competent professional person should be sought.

Library of Congress Cataloging-in-Publication Data

Names: Janove, Jathan, 1958- author.
Title: Hard-won wisdom : true stories from the management trenches / Jathan
  Janove.
Description: New York City : AMACOM, 2016.
Identifiers: LCCN 2016024567| ISBN 9780814437773 (paperback) | ISBN
  9780814437803 (ebook)
Subjects: LCSH: Supervision of employees. | Problem solving. |
  Employees--Rating of.
Classification: LCC HF5549.12 .J36 2016 | DDC 658.3--dc23 LC record available at
https://lccn.loc.gov/2016024567

About AMA
American Management Association (www.amanet.org) is a world leader in talent development, advancing the skills of individuals to drive business success. Our mission is to support the goals of individuals and organizations through a complete range of products and services, including classroom and virtual seminars, webcasts, webinars, podcasts, conferences, corporate and government solutions, business books, and research. AMA's approach to improving performance combines experiential learning—learning through doing—with opportunities for ongoing professional growth at every step of one's career journey

10 9 8 7 6 5 4 3 2 1

To my incredible wife and best friend, Marjorie —
Since December 1978, you've been the #1 source
of encouragement for my written work. Thank you!

ACKNOWLEGMENTS

This book was made possible by many people who were instrumental in my career. In 1991, while my wife Marjorie was at home with our three young children, I left a secure partnership in an established law firm to pursue my dream of creating my own labor and employment law practice. Thankfully, the late Steve Beeley, President of the Utah Employers Council, stepped in. Despite his outspoken antipathy to lawyers and the legal system, Steve took a liking to this "somewhat tolerable young lawyer." His introductions created the foundation of my new firm. My regret is that I never fully expressed my gratitude before an automobile accident tragically cut short Steve's life.

As monumental as Steve's contributions were, others played extremely helpful roles. Undoubtedly, the passage of time and the imperfections of my memory will produce important omissions. Nevertheless, here's a list of those I can recall in alphabetical order: Lois Baar, Jim Barrett, Debbie Bell, Cate Burns, Dan Cooper, Larry Ferguson, Dan Miller, Lloyd Fishman, Jim Greenbaum, Pam Hitt, Mark Holland, Elaine House, Paul Jones, Louonna Kachur, Rod Lacey, Eleanor Lovland, Charlotte Miller, Roy Montclair, Rob Moore, George Myers, Max Neves, Mike O'Brien, Scott Parson, Carol Bales Schnipper, Rich Stayner, Bob Waggoner, Monica Whalen and Darin Wilson. I also include two others who are no longer with us:

Mike Walton, whose brilliance was as outsized as his heart, and Don Wheeler, as kind a human being as you could ever meet.

In addition to those who've helped me build a rewarding professional practice, others have been very helpful in improving and refining my written work. They include: Hera Arsen, Maria Danaher, Christina Folz, Howard Heitner, Jim Isaacson, Raphael Janove, Stephen S. Power, Allen Smith and Robert White.

Words escape my feelings of gratitude. Thank you! Thank you!! Thank you!!!

CONTENTS

PREFACE

To build a collection of workplace stories for managers to learn from, I can't think of a better way than a career in employment law. You get a ringside seat for just about every form of workplace behavior you could ever imagine (or would prefer not to imagine.)

My professional experience began in 1980 as a first-year law student at the University of Chicago. I got a full-time summer job working in the employment-discrimination section of a legal aid clinic. The job continued during school years on a part-time basis. My clients were women and minorities who brought harassment, discrimination, and retaliation claims against their employers.

I vividly recall my very first client. Tall, handsome, and athletically built, he showed up at the clinic claiming he'd been fired as a hospital orderly due to national origin discrimination.

"What reason did the hospital give you?" I asked.

"They said I was fondling female patients."

"Were you?" I asked.

"It depends what you mean by 'fondling.'"

I thought to myself, "The guy lost his orderly job and now thinks he's a lawyer." I said, "Other than as a necessary part of your job duties, did you touch any patient's private parts, whether on top of or underneath their clothing?"

"Some of them, sure," he replied.

"Well," I said, trying to look as lawyerly as a first-year law student can look who still had pimples, "that would most likely be deemed 'fondling.'"

"But they asked me to!"

Trying to avoid sarcasm, I explained that consensual fondling of hospital patients would most likely be considered outside his job description. I asked, "What makes you think your national origin had something to do with your being fired?"

"I don't know if it's that," he said, "but it just doesn't seem fair." He added, "It might be something else that I know was held against me."

"What's that?" I asked.

"My good looks," he said.

"Huh?"

"My ex-boss is short, fat, and ugly. He used to make comments like, 'You must be quite the ladies man.' Or, 'Here comes the stud.' I think he resented me because I was the best looking guy there, and he's ugly."

I ended up telling the ex-orderly that he didn't have a very good case and suggested he drop the claim and spend his time finding another job. I explained that the categories of workers protected under federal and state antidiscrimination laws had not yet been expanded to include handsome ladies' men. That would be a burden he'd have to shoulder himself.

Another client taught third grade in the Chicago public school system. One year, Mr. Johnson's class included an especially hyperactive boy. The child increasingly got on my client's nerves. One day, after the boy was at his disruptive worst and refused to return to his seat, Mr. Johnson picked him up and threw him into the chalkboard.

Although he didn't lift the child over his head and toss him World Wrestling Federation style, the impact caused a small cut on the boy's ear.

The school responded by firing him. Mr. Johnson's internal appeals to the school board were denied. As a result, he came to our clinic for representation. I took his case to court.

Because there had been a big outcry by parents, including the Parent Teachers Association, the school board took this case very seriously. My opponent was a distinguished, silver-haired veteran of the bar who was probably older than my father. His monogrammed shirt probably cost more than my suit, shirt, tie, and shoes put together (but not my law school tuition!).

The hearing took place in a musty courtroom in downtown Chicago. The judge had an unusually large head and was nicknamed "Moose," although no one dared call him that.

Somewhat nervously, I looked up at Judge Moose in his black robe and conceded that throwing a third grader into a chalkboard wasn't desirable teacher behavior. But I then proclaimed, "However, Your Honor, my client's conduct does not merit career capital punishment!"

I argued that since Mr. Johnson was the only teacher in the school who was a minority—the other teachers, the principal, the students, and the parents were white—race must have influenced "this rush to judgment against my client."

You might think my argument flimsy, but not Judge Moose. He ordered that Mr. Johnson be reinstated with full teaching privileges. But like King Solomon, Judge Moose split the baby. He ordered reinstatement without back pay. "That will be punishment enough," he said.

On the way out of the courtroom, the silver-haired school board attorney pulled me aside. "Son," he said, "nice job. Now find out your client's price and give me a call. We're prepared to pay whatever it takes for him to go away." He then clutched my elbow. Looking me in the eye, he said, "Understand one thing. Your client will *never* teach in our school system again. *Never.*"

I shared this conversation with Mr. Johnson and added what I thought was his good economic fortune under the circumstances. "You can get a substantial sum of money right now to tide you over while you find a teaching job elsewhere," I said. "And I'm sure they'll agree to give you a neutral reference as part of the deal. On the other hand, if you insist on reinstatement, they'll fight you in court for years and you could easily lose."

Mr. Johnson's reaction surprised me. "How dare you suggest such a thing? I'm in the right! They must return me to my classroom! Maybe what I need is a real lawyer. Not some kid."

Ouch! So much for ego gratification.

After experiences like these—representing a consensual patient fondler and a self-righteous third-grader thrower—a sensible person might have switched from employment law to something more sane and sober like tax law. But I was hooked, including on studying why people in the workplace do what they do.

For this book I've selected 46 stories about how to behave in today's workplace and how not to behave. The stories come from (1) my former career as a labor and employment law litigator, (2) my subsequent work as an organizational consultant, executive coach, and workplace leadership trainer, and (3) personal experiences, including as a manager. Topics run the gamut: hiring, firing, performance management, employee engagement, succession planning, conflict resolution, documentation, information flow, harassment, discrimination, and downsizing. Although these stories are based on real events, to protect people's privacy, I've changed not only names but other details as well. Other than myself, I don't identify anyone directly or indirectly, and any resemblance should be deemed coincidental. Also, the "moral of the stories" is not intended as legal advice.

Some stories will resonate with you more than others. Perhaps it will be the glass-eating trial lawyer who cringes at the thought of confronting his secretary ("Tough Trial Lawyer Turns Timid"). Or the email-addicted CEO who decides to fire his CFO ("Discharge from 4 Doors Down"). Or perhaps it will be a story about one of my own professional missteps ("The Stupid Switch, Part One"). Maybe it will be a communications tool you find especially valuable, such as the Same Day Summary ("'Texas Wes' and the Same Day Summary"), the Star Profile ("Beating the Coin Toss"), or Verbal Aikido ("A Midnight Encounter at a Portland Pub.")

You can read the book cover to cover, select sections, pick story titles that grab your attention, or just let the book fall open and start reading. However you approach reading the book, my goal is to provide you leadership, communication, and management concepts and tools you'll use to good effect. After each story you'll find a moral that will help you apply its lessons to your own workplace.

All managers have the ability and the opportunity to step up their game. I hope this book helps accomplish that result for you.

CHAPTER

1

EMPLOYEE ENGAGEMENT

AN AFFIRMATIVE ACTION THAT WORKED
(A Changed Approach to Managing Employees Produces Dramatically Better Results)

Chuck, a white male, desperately wanted to fire Mary, an African American female.

As head of his company's accounting department, Chuck had become increasingly frustrated with Mary's performance and attitude. He had established a program, the Call List, which involved department employees checking in with customers every 60 days. The list was divided evenly among the five employees in Chuck's department. Unlike her coworkers, Mary regularly fell short of completing her share of the calls.

When Chuck spoke to her about the problem, Mary became defensive and made excuses. Their relationship deteriorated, with Mary becoming less and less engaged and Chuck becoming more and more frustrated. At one point, Chuck became angry with Mary and vented his frustration. Mary became upset and pointedly observed that perhaps he had a problem with her race since everyone else in the department was white.

Chuck backed off and for a time let the performance issues slide. Eventually, however, Chuck reached the point where he'd had enough—Mary had to go!

To fire Mary, he needed a sign-off from the human resources director, Betty. However, Betty noted the lack of documentation in Mary's personnel file and absence of progressive discipline. She also noted inconsistencies, including favorable performance appraisals Mary had received. Chuck explained, "I didn't want a big argument or to have her accuse me of anything so I checked the necessary boxes to keep the peace."

Based on this record, Betty refused to support a termination, which further frustrated Chuck. He continued to press his case, which led to my being brought in for a second opinion as the company's employment attorney.

I agreed with Betty, which made Chuck mad at me. "This is all a bunch of politically correct garbage!" he said. "Between HR and the lawyers, a manager can't manage. And there's not a damn thing you can do about it!"

"Yes, there is something you can do," I said.

"What?"

"Change the way you manage employees," I said.

"I want legal advice!" Chuck practically shouted.

"I'm giving it to you," I said.

Chuck's unhappiness with the status quo created an opportunity for change. Incentivized by the thought of being able to fire Mary, he agreed to create what I call Star Profiles for the positions in his department and use them to increase employee engagement, or to determine if an employee doesn't belong, which Chuck assumed would be the case with Mary.

I helped Chuck come up with a short, tight, action-oriented word picture of the most important things Mary and her coworkers could do to be successful—what would make the most meaningful difference in their performance. After some thought and discussion, Chuck came up with a three-sentence profile that captured the behavior of successful accounting department employees:

1. Record and transmit every transaction promptly and accurately.
2. Diligently complete the Call List to improve account handling and customer relations.
3. Help build a working environment based on trust, respect, and cooperation.

Next, Chuck held meetings with each of his five employees, explaining these three core behaviors, why they were necessary to the accounting department's success, and inviting their ideas and suggestions on how to best achieve them. He followed up with short written summaries of the key points of each discussion and scheduled follow-up meetings.

Initially, Chuck balked at having to make this effort with his four "good" employees. "If it ain't broke, why fix it?"

Betty and I explained that Mary needed a fair opportunity to succeed, which included being treated consistently with her coworkers. "Plus," I said, "you may be in for a pleasant surprise."

Sure enough, Chuck unexpectedly discovered that his effort to crystallize and communicate the most valuable things his employees could do improved the other four employees' performance. Chuck said, "They were good before, but now I've got some of the best employees in the whole company!"

Chuck's biggest surprise, however, came with Mary.

I hadn't heard anything for nearly a year when Betty and Chuck called me. They had another disagreement. And it was about Mary. She had submitted her notice of resignation, explaining that family issues required her to be away from work longer than was allowed under company policy.

Get this: Chuck wanted an exception to be made—in Mary's favor. Betty disagreed, citing the need for consistency.

"Is Mary requesting an exception?" I asked.

"No," Chuck said. "She said she fully understands and accepts the policy. In fact, she'd probably be embarrassed if she knew I was trying to make an exception for her."

"Then why are you doing it?" I asked.

"Because she's so good at her job! It would be a shame to lose her."

"Besides," Chuck added, "she's one of the few black employees we have in the company. Can't we make an exception for this reason?"

Betty and I explained to Chuck that this would not be a good idea. We suggested that instead of violating company policy, he should stay in touch with Mary after she left and invite her to reapply once her family issues were resolved.

This story highlights the enormous potential that exists in nearly every workplace relationship yet tragically is so often missed. Consider the irony: The manager who desperately wanted to fire an employee but felt race prevented it was now seeking an exception to company policy to retain that same employee—and trying to use race to justify it.

After Chuck shifted his attention from what frustrated him to identifying and describing the actions and behavior that would produce the greatest value, the dynamic in his relationship with his employees changed. Instead of top-down, hierarchal, "I'm the boss" leadership, Chuck created the opportunity for collaboration—how each member of his department could individually and collectively contribute to the greater good. As a result, good employees became better. Their performance increased with their engagement level.

As for Mary, Chuck's new approach effectively hit the reset button. She felt an enormous weight lifted off of her shoulders, which was the feeling that her boss was out to get her, possibly because of her race. The three sentences of her profile provided a roadmap for Mary's success: a clear sense of the importance of her job; how it contributed to the department, the company, and customers; and how she could make a meaningful difference. As a result, Mary began bringing a level of energy and dedication to her job Chuck had not previously seen.

For people reporting to you, what actions are most needed for success? I'm not talking about a fantasy wish list or a run-on laundry list of qualifications. Star Profiles are succinct, action-oriented statements of what's most important. They're not mini-descriptions of jobs. They're invitations to an ongoing, collaborative relationship that gives employees a sense of purpose, creates daily opportunities to make a difference, and connects them to their boss and each other as human beings.

Note: The Star Profile concept is covered in the chapter 2 stories "Beating the Coin Toss," "The Professor Has a Close Call," and "The Succession Scramble Sinks," and the chapter 3 story "Course Correction or Corrective Action?"

A SALE THAT FAILED
(Don't Risk Disengaging Your Employees
by Keeping Them Out of the Loop)

With some trepidation, Cheryl agreed to support her husband's dream. As a result, John quit his position as a senior computer engineer at a large company in Chicago, took out a second mortgage on their home, and started his own consulting business.

The new company struggled for a while but eventually turned a profit. John's 90-hour workweeks began to pay off. He developed a loyal group of clients and a network of talented consultants.

Over the years, John developed a trusted lieutenant. An athletically built man in his mid-30s, Brad was as devoted to the company as he was to his boss. He combined a fierce sense of pride and loyalty. Sometimes passion got the better of him. However, the results he produced were consistently impressive.

As the business grew, John saw an opportunity to expand and open a second office in another state. He said to Brad, "What about opening and managing an office in St. Louis? I think you and the company would thrive."

Without hesitation, Brad replied, "I'm ready. Let's do it!"

Over the next several years, the St. Louis office grew to where it rivaled the Chicago office in revenue and profitability. By now, John had paid off both mortgages. He'd become financially well off.

Cheryl began to talk to John about *her* dream. It involved him retiring while the two were in good health and could travel and spend quality time with their children and grandchildren. John agreed, saying he was getting tired of his marathon workweeks. He added his own desire: to buy a sailboat they could use to explore places like the Caribbean and the San Juan Islands.

John approached a business broker who said the market was ripe for a company like his to be sold. The broker began preparing a prospectus to give to potential buyers.

John faced a dilemma. "What do I tell Brad?" he asked himself. Unfortunately, he chose not to tell Brad anything. John reasoned to himself, "Brad is a great guy and has been indispensable, but he can get emotional and sometimes unpredictable. It's better he not know what's going on for now. Once I've got a deal in place, I'll show him how well he'll be taken care of."

Time went by while Brad continued to build up the St. Louis operation. However, he began to notice that John had become less talkative about the future of the company. At one point Brad asked him, "John, are you selling the company?"

John replied, "Why no. I haven't offered to sell the company to anybody." John rationalized to himself that his statement was technically true since no offers had yet been made. However, he left out the part about retaining a broker.

A few months later, a large Asian company offered to buy John's company at an extremely attractive price. The deal would include a large retention bonus and substantial raise for Brad as head of the St. Louis office. John also planned to sweeten the deal by giving Brad a generous personal "thank you" payment from John's share of the profits.

The deal on the table meant John and Cheryl's retirement dream would be fully funded. The deal just needed to close. However, with the closing two weeks away, John received an email from the buyer's representatives: "Before completing this transaction, we would like to meet the manager of your St. Louis office since he will be an important part of the company going forward. We are in New York this week and request that he meet us there."

This message threw John into a state of panic. He jumped on a plane to St. Louis, carrying plane tickets to New York for himself and Brad.

With sweaty palms, John opened the front door of the St. Louis office. "Hi Brad," he said.

His eyes wide in surprise, Brad said, "What are you doing in town? I had no idea you were coming."

"Brad, I need to speak with you in private. Let's go downstairs to the coffee shop."

Seated at a corner table, John explained what had been happening. Brad's reaction was not positive: "What?! You sold the company! Without telling me?!"

Brad remembered John's earlier denial of selling the company and added, "In fact, you lied to me!"

John started to explain that his statement had been "technically true" at the time, but Brad cut him off. "You sent me to St. Louis, and I built this operation from scratch. I busted my butt for you for twelve years and that's how you treat me!"

"But Brad, you'll be well rewarded. There will be a substantial retention bonus and salary increase. Also, I plan to write you a sizable check myself. You'll still be fully in charge of the St. Louis office. These changes will be good for you."

"Don't give me that crap," Brad replied acidly. "You just want me to play nice so that Asian outfit pays you a boatload of money and makes you rich. Don't insult my intelligence with a bunch of BS about how much you care about me!"

The rest of their meeting did not go much better. However, Brad eventually agreed to fly with John to New York to meet the buyer's representatives.

At the meeting, John introduced Brad to the others. At first, Brad was polite, although not very communicative. John tried drawing Brad out into a discussion of the St. Louis operation, its many successes, and future growth opportunities. Brad started to open up a bit.

One of the buyer's representatives said, "We are pleased to have you work for us Brad. Your boss negotiated hard on your behalf to make us pay you a lot of money. But he promises we will get a good return on our investment." The representative added, "You have a very loyal boss."

The last comment was too much for Brad. "Oh yeah, John's a hell of a loyal boss," he said sarcastically. "You can't do better than good old John when it comes to loyalty."

John's cheeks flushed as Brad continued, "As for your 'return on investment,' as you call it, who do you think built the St. Louis operation? John? Please! I did it myself while he sat back in Chicago counting his money."

"Easy Brad," John said. "This is a win-win situation here. No need to get angry."

"Who's angry?" Brad replied hotly. "I just want to make sure our Asian friends understand the facts, including that if I were to leave the company, the St. Louis office would fall to pieces. I don't need to hear a bunch of crap about their getting a 'return on investment!'"

The rest of the room fell silent. But Brad wasn't done. "I'm not impressed with your offer," he said to the buyer's representatives. "You know, maybe I should start my own business. You guys wouldn't stand a chance competing against me."

"But Brad," John stammered, "you've got a noncompete contract. You can't do that."

Brad stared directly at John. "So sue me," he said, with a sneer. With that, Brad walked out of the room, slammed the door behind him, and went downstairs to catch the next flight to St. Louis.

After Brad left, the buyer's representatives said they needed to speak with each other in private and asked John to leave the room. After about ten minutes, they called him in. Apologetically, they said to an ashen-faced John, "We are very sorry, but we are afraid your company no longer fits our acquisition guidelines. We wish you success in finding another buyer."

The next two years were very difficult for John. After firing Brad, he assumed management responsibilities for St. Louis as well as Chicago. Instead of enjoying retirement with Cheryl, his workweek hours increased as he commuted regularly to St. Louis, desperately trying to preserve the business while finding another buyer. In addition, he had to fight a pitched legal battle with Brad over the noncompete agreement as well as Brad's own claim of breach of contract.

Eventually the legal issues were resolved and another buyer found. However, the price paid for John's business was less than half of what the Asian company had offered two years earlier.

What I most remember is the point when John described the impact on Cheryl. His eyes filled with tears and his voice caught. He shook his head sadly and said, "This was supposed to be her dream too."

MORAL OF THE STORY

John had an understandable fear of sharing sensitive information with his employee. But his instinct to withhold information actually led to the very thing he feared most. Without realizing it, John sowed the seeds of mistrust. It also led to his rationalized "rational lie," stating a technical truth he knew to be misleading. In doing so, he unwittingly set the stage for the disastrous meeting in New York. No amount of money would assuage Brad's feeling of being deceived by his boss. John's instinct to withhold information created a terrible environment for the time when that information had to be shared. Instead of engaging his most valuable employee in the sale, John converted him into an actively disengaged employee who sank the deal.

Of course, sharing sensitive information should be done with preparation and care. There may be circumstances when withholding information from employees is appropriate. However, the presumption should be to share the information with those to whom it would be important, not withhold it.

Imagine if John had sat down with Brad early in the process and said:

"Brad, I've been doing a lot of thinking lately. Like you, I'm a workaholic. Cheryl's had to keep the house, raise the kids, and tend to aging parents without much help from me. Yet she supported me when I left a secure job to pursue my dream of starting my own company.

"Well, Cheryl has a dream of her own. It's that I retire while we're both still in good health so that we can travel and get to know our grandchildren. And I've also got my own little dream, which is to buy a sailboat and spend a lot of time on it.

"With your support, we've built a great business over the years. But I'm starting to get tired. A business broker told me the market is right to sell to one of the big players in our industry. With what we've saved over the years, Cheryl and I can establish a comfortable retirement if we sell in this current market.

"I'd like your help in making this dream a reality."

Courtesy of the U.S. legal system, I got to know Brad—via deposition taking, mediation, and other proceedings. Based on what I learned about Brad, I have no doubt in stating what his response would have been had John conveyed a message like the one above. John wouldn't have needed to add the part about Brad being well compensated. Considering Brad's fierce pride and loyalty, as well as his zealous devotion to results, Brad's wheels would have been turning instantly. "I'm going to deliver one final victory for John and Cheryl!"

If you want to keep your employees engaged, when it comes to sharing versus withholding information, here are the questions to ask yourself:

- If I were in the employees' shoes, what would I want to know?
- If I keep this information to myself, what are the potential negative consequences?
- If the information is potentially problematic for my employees, what can I say or do to minimize negative reaction?

"SHE'S ACTUALLY PLEASANT!"
(Recognition of Positive Behavior Produces More of the Same)

Many years ago, I founded and managed a law firm. I employed a receptionist, Gladys. In her 50s with a prior career in the military, Gladys was intelligent, reliable—and a bit sharp around the edges. When interacting with others, she had a suffer-no-fools manner.

Gladys was so good at the other aspects of the job that I overlooked the rough edges. At least, that was my excuse.

One day, Gladys put a call through to me while I was in my office.

"Jathan," she said. "Your client Bill is on line two. Do you want to take the call?"

"Yes," I said. "Please put it through."

(Note to millennials: This was in the old days.)

During my conversation with Bill, he said something un-related to the legal matter we were discussing. "What's up with Gladys?" he asked.

"I don't know," I said. "What do you mean?"

In a surprised tone, he said, "She was actually quite pleasant on the telephone."

I had no explanation for her unusual behavior and fin-ished the conversation.

Having recently given a presentation about positive em-ployee recognition, it struck me that now would be a good time to practice what I preached. I got up from my desk and walked out of my office to the reception area.

"Gladys," I said.

"Yes?"

"I was just on the phone with Bill, and—"

Gladys cut me off. "Well duh," she said. "Don't you think I know that? Who do you think put the call into you?"

(As you can see, Gladys's suffer-no-fools style meant suffer *no* fools—even if the fool was the boss.)

"My bad," I said. "Of course you knew that. Anyway, I

just wanted to tell you that Bill said you were very pleasant on the phone."

Gladys didn't say anything in response. However, I observed a faint blush on her neck and face.

Thereafter, as I and others in the office noticed, when Gladys answered the phone, there was a degree of warmth not detected before.

MORAL OF THE STORY

This story illustrates the power of direct recognition of behavior a manager thinks is worth repeating. Our brains are wired in such a way that when someone—especially someone in a position of authority—positively recognizes an action we've taken or result we've obtained, we want to do more of the same.

Unfortunately, managers generally do a lousy job of giving recognition. (For years, I was no exception.) There are several reasons why. Their own bosses were probably not good role models. Managers are busy, and giving recognition takes time; it's easier to take positive behavior for granted. Besides, isn't that what their paycheck is for?

I tell managers who think and act this way, "You're leaving money on the table. You're missing out on quick, easy opportunities to get more of what *you* want: productivity, reliability, quality, initiative, and accountability. Highly engaged employees give you that. A boss's direct recognition of positive behavior links the employee to a shared purpose, underscores the difference the employee is making, and connects the two of you as human beings. That spells engagement."

Think about it from a business standpoint. Assume you were the owner of my firm, Janove & Associates. Profits went into your pocket, and losses came out of it. Would Gladys's behavior change matter to you? How about in your business? Does customer service matter?

Yet did I "command and control" this positive behavior change? Did I rely on a job description? Did I fall on bended knee and beg, "Please, Gladys, be nicer on the phone. Please!" No. Direct recognition of behavior worth repeating is powerful stuff. Make a habit of it and get ready to smile at the results.

To get started, I recommend the following exercise. Reflect on the things your employees do that are worth repeating, whether major or minor. These could relate to productivity, reliability, flexibility, initiative, treatment of others, safety, quality, team play, or anything else you value. List in writing as many things as you can think of. Turn to this list at least twice a workday, once in the morning to prime you to give recognition and once at the end of the day to reflect on how well you did.

Here's another thing you can do: Get a battery and put it on your desk or otherwise keep it present. Why? Because batteries have two terminals. The negative terminal is to remind you not to let employee problems fester, a topic I'll cover in chapter 3, "Performance Management." The positive terminal is your behavior prompt to give recognition instead of taking positive behavior for granted.

Now, if you're an environmentally conscientious type, no worries (we have lots of them in the Pacific Northwest). Instead of getting a battery, get a *picture* of a battery—preferably on fully biodegradable, recyclable paper.

A COSTLY LOST OPPORTUNITY
(Unexpected Gestures of Recognition Are Especially Powerful)

Before I had my own firm, I worked in other law firms. In one of these firms, a young, ambitious attorney came to us with a vision. Max wanted to create a specialty law practice he felt was largely untapped and could be extremely lucrative. He said he needed two years to put all of his time and effort in building up a referral network and other resources that would make this new practice a reality.

We were impressed with his pitch and negotiated a two-year deal. We agreed to pay him a modest salary while exempting him from all firm, client, and other responsibilities.

As the two years neared an end, the cost of Max's salary, overhead, and professional support still exceeded the revenue he'd thus far brought in. However, it was obvious that he'd laid the foundation of what would be a long-term highly profitable practice.

At the year-end meeting to approve distribution of annual profits, one of the partners, Dave, said, "I propose we give Max a $5,000 bonus."

"Why?" asked another partner. "We're still in the red on him."

"I know," said Dave. "But does anyone doubt the kind of revenue that will soon be flowing into the firm?"

Another partner spoke up:

"I agree that Max has done an outstanding job and the firm will eventually do extremely well. However, that's when we should give him a bonus, not now. He hasn't asked for a bonus and isn't expecting one. He made it clear he only wanted a modest salary and administrative support. He said he'd talk to us about a new deal once we've gotten back our investment."

Dave said:

"It's precisely because he isn't expecting a bonus that we should do it. He will be totally surprised and probably try to refuse it. But we should insist. We've had an excellent year financially. We can easily afford to take $5,000 out of the pot and give it to Max."

"Okay Dave," another partner said jokingly, "we'll take it out of *your* share." Several partners laughed.

The partners took a vote. Dave's proposal went down in defeat.

Years later, after I'd left the firm, one of my former partners told me that once the revenue did roll in and Max had repaid the firm's investment, he drove a hard bargain about his compensation going forward. "Basically," this partner said, "Max made it clear he'd leave the firm unless we agreed to treat his practice as a business within a business. This meant that while we got something out of the deal, it wasn't that great. Max took the lion's share."

Subsequently, I bumped into Max at a community event. We scheduled lunch.

After we met and ordered our food, I couldn't contain my curiosity. I asked Max about what happened after he'd turned the corner on his new practice.

"I told the managing partner, 'It's time for a new deal,'" Max said. "He responded by saying the firm would make me a partner and that given how strong my numbers were, I'd do well in their system.

"I told him I didn't want to be paid under the firm's system. I wanted my own system. I'd built this business on my own and it was entirely dependent on me."

Max continued:

"The managing partner looked at me in surprise. Hard bargaining followed. Things reached the point where I made plans to leave, including having a lease drawn up for space in another building, obtaining a bank loan, and putting together a network of attorneys to work for me. I went to the managing partner and told him I planned to leave and take the business with me.

"He said, 'Wait a minute. Let me talk to the partnership.'

"Evidently the prospect of my leaving changed their perspective because we got a deal done that's still in place."

At the conclusion of lunch, I told Max about the partnership meeting years before and Dave's unsuccessful effort to obtain a $5,000 bonus for him. Max hadn't known anything about it. He hadn't expected a bonus then and wasn't disappointed when he didn't get one.

"I'd probably have voted against Dave, too," he said.

"Max," I said, "let's assume the partnership had told you it wanted you to accept a $5,000 bonus because it had complete confidence in your eventual success and wanted to make a gesture of appreciation."

"I probably would have declined it," Max said. "I hadn't earned it yet."

"What if we'd insisted and perhaps added a condition that you not use the money for ordinary expenses but something special, like a family vacation or contribution to your kids' college education fund?"

Before Max could answer, I added with a smile, "Let me put it another way Max. Let's say we did something like that back then. In terms of the deal you ultimately negotiated with the firm, the hard bargaining you described, how much money would that $5,000 gesture have cost you long term?"

"I don't know," Max said. Then he slowly shook his head, chuckled, and said with a big smile, "You know, I'd rather not even think about it."

MORAL OF THE STORY

The earlier story, about Gladys the receptionist, emphasized words of recognition; this one focused on gestures. When we do something for someone that's not expected, the impact can be powerful.

It doesn't have to be money, and it doesn't have to be substantial. Just something affirmative to show you value the person's contributions and care about him or her. The gesture could be a gift card, a handwritten note, a meal, a bottle of wine, or something creative like what a friend of mine does, sending people customized cards with personalized pictures.

The impact of these gestures isn't limited to compensation negotiations as in Max's case. Consider employee retention. When talented people leave your organization, do you rely on what they tell you in exit interviews? Typically, it's a partial truth: "The pay will be better," "The commute will be shorter," "There's better growth opportunity," etc. What's missing is what made the employee return the headhunter's call, follow up on the Internet job inquiry, or otherwise consider alternative employment possibilities. What's also missing is why they never told you their plans until it was too late to retain them. Had you asked them how appreciated they felt at work, and had they answered honestly, I predict the answer would not have been encouraging.

Max's law firm was perfectly justified in not giving him a bonus. They had a deal: a modest paycheck and administrative support in exchange for Max having two years of freedom to build his new practice. The firm kept its end of the bargain as did Max.

In other words, their relationship was transactional. It was an arm's-length exchange between two parties as opposed to a bond formed between human beings. This meant that once the first deal ended and Max held the leverage, he could negotiate as good a deal for himself as possible without qualms or guilt pangs.

Most workplace relationships are transactional. From the employee's perspective, it's, "I put in my time and do my job in exchange for the money and benefits I get." From the manager's perspective, it's, "I give the instructions, and assuming my employees follow them, they keep their jobs and continue to get their pay." Transactional relationships are self-focused versus other-focused. They're functional but not engaged.

If you want to move from functional to engaged, I suggest adding gestures to your words of appreciation.

IF YOU WANT ENGAGEMENT, LEAD BY LISTENING
(What's Your Period/Question-Mark Ratio?)

As an executive coach, I was working with Phil, director of finance for his company. He shared frustrations he was having with one of his staff accountants, Melinda. She wasn't performing to his expectations, yet he struggled communicating with her. "She gets defensive so easily," he said. "I have trouble speaking with her about performance issues. I feel like we are pulling in opposite directions."

I suggested that as clearly and specifically as he could, Phil should explain his performance expectations, including the reasons. I also encouraged him to frame his communications in a go-forward, future-looking, positive way.

I suggested we do a role play. Pretending I was Melinda, I said, "You've come to my office. I invite you in and you sit down. Now speak."

Phil proceeded to lay out each of his expectations in great detail, providing reasons for each, and identifying gaps in Melinda's performance with those expectations. Phil then articulated specific solutions by which Melinda could close these gaps.

He finished and looked at me for approval.

"You did a very thorough job of explaining the current situation," I said. "You explained what needed to change, why, and how. You were specific and detailed without being judgmental. You didn't dwell on the past but focused on the future, including how Melinda could succeed.

"Your message was terrific except for one thing."

"What's that?" Phil asked.

I showed Phil a picture of a large period and a large question mark with a ratio sign between them. "Do you know what this is?" I asked.

"I'm not sure," Phil replied.

"It symbolizes the Period/Question-Mark Ratio. When

you're conversing with your employees, for every one of your sentences that ends in a period, how many end with question marks?"

"I never thought about it," Phil said.

"What would you estimate?"

"I don't know."

"How about just now in the role play where I was Melinda?"

"Beats me," Phil said. "Probably more periods than question marks."

"You're a numbers guy," I said. "What's the symbol for infinity? I counted over a dozen sentences without a single one ending in a question mark."

"That bad?" he said.

"It's not that it's bad, it's just a missed opportunity. You did a terrific job of laying out the facts. Now to really engage Melinda, you need to blend in questions. Invite her to be part of the process."

I taught Phil the "EAR" method of listening, where "E" stands for "explore," which means asking open-ended, exploratory questions; "A" is for "acknowledge," by which the listener confirms his or her understanding with the speaker; and after the speaker confirms that the listener's understanding is correct, the listener "responds," the "R."

After some practice, Phil built questions into his planned discussion with Melinda. What did she think? How did she see things? What did she see as a solution? "How can I [Phil] help you succeed?"

The results? Very soon a low-trust, low-engagement relationship turned into high trust, high engagement. And Phil became a devotee of leading through questions.

MORAL OF THE STORY

In "An Employee Engagement Lesson Learned from a Volunteer Experience," two stories down, I identify three pillars of engaged workplace relationships: (1) making a difference, (2) sharing a purpose, and (3) connecting personally. I can think of no better way to support all three than developing a habit of asking employees questions and listening to their answers.

The Period/Question-Mark Ratio and EAR method form an excellent one-two combination. The first is for self-awareness. It's a check-in. I'll find myself speaking to someone when a little voice inside my head whispers, "What's your ratio Jathan?" I'll make a quick count. If it's skewed toward periods (my wife would say a not-unusual circumstance), I'll stop and ask a question instead of making another statement.

The EAR supplies the methodology. Its three parts are normally done in sequence.

1. Start by exploring the other person's position, asking open-ended questions such as, "What do you think?," "How do you see it?," "What are some examples?"

2. Move to acknowledgment, confirming your understanding of what the person thinks is important: "So if I understand you . . . Is that accurate?" "So your main concern is . . . Is that right?"
3. After the person confirms that you understand what matters, respond.

Why Is the EAR Method Effective?

1. It improves the quality of your response. Instead of shooting from the hip, following the EAR sequence will give you the information and time to craft a nuanced, intelligent response.
2. At the psychological level, the "E" and the "A" combine to create a receptive environment for communication. Think about how you felt the last time someone heard your point of view and showed he or she had paid attention and understood. You felt pretty good, didn't you?
3. The EAR method eliminates perhaps the number one culprit in relationship breakdown: the erroneous assumption. Far too often, we jump to our response, basing it on what we assume about the other person. We shouldn't be surprised that our response elicits a negative reaction—its inaccuracy offends the other person, who feels misunderstood.

The EAR listening method is useful in essentially all exchanges. However, it's especially useful in building engaged relationships. You can use it to create a shared sense of purpose by asking employees what they think is most important. You can help them enjoy a greater sense of accomplishment by asking them what will make them more effective in their jobs. And simply by using this method, you will create a stronger personal connection with your employees.

The EAR method isn't a rigid, mechanical tool. Rather, it's an approach to keep you other-focused versus self-focused and maximize the likelihood of your having positive, constructive relationships with your employees.

"MANAGING MILLENNIALS IS THE PITS!"
(Boomers and Xers Create Self-Fulfilling Prophecies)

Sam was in his 50s and ran his company's marketing department. He called me one day to vent his frustration. "What's wrong with these millennials?" he said. "They frustrate the hell out of me!"

"What do you mean?" I asked.

"First of all, they have no loyalty," he said. "It's here today, gone tomorrow. Second, their work ethic is lousy. They're too caught up in their own personal worlds. And third, they don't know how to communicate. It's probably because they've spent their lives on their various electronic gizmos!"

If Sam expected sympathy, he didn't get it.

"Let's take your charges in order," I said.

"Charge number one, lack of loyalty. How much loyalty do you expect? Millennials grew up during the Great Recession. They probably had parents who lost their jobs or feared losing them. Today, they work in the era of mounting college debt that's not offset by attractive career options.

"Employers continually strive to do more with less. They proclaim, 'Our employees come first,' yet when times get tough, 'first' usually means 'out the door.' In many workplaces, new hires start off receiving lengthy handbooks, sets of rules they're told to obey subject to harsh consequences if they don't. They get lectured on avoiding harassment and other misbehavior and are pointedly reminded they're 'at will,' meaning they can be fired whenever the employer feels like it. How's that for a welcome? Frankly, the term *onboarding* reminds me of another kind of 'boarding.'

"Charge number two, poor work ethic/self-absorption. Let's assume you're right. Are you satisfied with your efforts to tap their motivation? What are you doing to give them a sense of purpose, the belief that they're engaged in a cause that matters? Are you creating opportunities for them to make a difference and giving them recognition when they do? What's your What/Why Ratio? For every time you tell them what to do, how often do you tell them why, as in why it matters? And what are you doing to connect with them on a personal level, to make them think you understand or care about them as human beings? In other words, what kind of investment are you making from which you might expect a favorable return?

"Charge number three, poor communication skills. On this one, I'm afraid millennials don't have the market cornered. Managers of all generations are guilty of undercommunicating, overcommunicating, or miscommunicating. Here's one way you might change this: Engage them in a conversation about how their familiarity with those "electronic gizmos" might help your company or department. Perhaps your millennials could bring innovation to the table that older, less-gizmo-oriented people might miss. Also, I understand your marketing efforts include millennials as potential customers, especially as they age and their purchasing power increases. Your millennial employees may be an untapped resource on how to maximize this potential. You just have to reach out and tap it."

I'm not going to say that after hearing my speech, Sam leaped to his feet and said, "Hallelujah! I see the light!" Nevertheless, it did get him thinking about what he might do differently that could produce better results. And he subsequently did say that millennial relations and results had gone up, while his frustration level had gone down.

MORAL OF THE STORY

I've heard many similar complaints about millennials from managers like Sam. They follow the same theme: Millennials aren't loyal, they're too self-focused, their work ethic is problematic, and they don't communicate well.

My response is always the same: Don't create self-fulfilling prophecies. The minute you indulge in the stereotypes, you're doomed to experience what you don't want.

A better idea is to use your millennials as a test case for the concepts and tools I'm sharing in this book. Start with the What/Why Ratio: Every time you tell an employee what to do, explain why, the purpose served by the action. Think of the alternative reference to millennials: Generation Y (as in the one that followed Generation X). Only think of it not as the letter *Y* but the word *why*. Make the What/Why Ratio 1:1 and watch what happens to the relationship.

Next, make the EAR method of listening a regular part of your management practice. Find topics of interest to your employees, including ones that involve their work as well as their lives away from work. Explore what matters to them while showing you've paid attention and actually listened.

Lastly, break the habit of taking positive employee behavior for granted. Make it a point to give direct recognition of behavior worth repeating. Periodically supplement your words of recognition with concrete gestures.

If you do these things, I make the following prediction: Within weeks, if not days, you'll say, "Who would have thought? These millennials aren't so bad."

AN EMPLOYEE-ENGAGEMENT LESSON LEARNED FROM A VOLUNTEER EXPERIENCE
(Employee Engagement Starts with Managers)

Motivated by the thought of helping feed needy families at holiday time, I volunteered to work a December Saturday at a local food bank.

That day was rice assembly. In a large warehouse-like room were placed a dozen or so rectangular metal tables. At each table, food-bank employees placed large vats of rice, which they periodically refilled during the day.

Teams of seven volunteers surrounded each table. Two people used plastic scoops to dip into the vat and pick up the prescribed amount of rice. Two baggers received the rice from the scoopers. One person put a twist tie around the neck of each bag. One person affixed a sticky label to the bottom of each bag. And one boxer counted out 19 bags, put them in a box, sealed it, and started a new one.

I was a scooper, and happy to be there. I worked diligently and energetically, experimenting with my scoop technique. Elbow in or elbow out? Supple wrist or stiff wrist? I strove to maximize my productivity.

Time flew until the other scooper left. He simply walked off the job and didn't return. His absence created a bottleneck on the rice assembly line.

I looked for a solution and found it. I grabbed the unused plastic scooper and, with a scooper in each hand, dipped both into the vat simultaneously, shoulder length apart. I moved each scooper toward the other on a collision course. Just before impact, I brought both up in a continuous motion. With a little practice, I was able to scoop and pour rice into the two baggers' bags at essentially the same rate as when we had two scoopers.

I had solved the problem, and I was engaged. Not only was I a scooper, I was an *inventor*, the creator of the "Janove Double-Scoop Technique."

Time flew until one of the baggers walked off the job and didn't return. Now we had a new problem: How do you utilize the Janove Double-Scoop Technique with only one bagger? Answer: You don't.

Again I looked for a solution and found it, or so I thought. I noticed that the labeler had taken advantage of the production lull to label bags in advance. She now had a large stack of prelabeled bags. So I said to her, "Hey, how about coming over here and filling in as a bagger?"

She looked at me coolly. "No," she said. "I'm a labeler. That's not my job."

Bereft of further ideas, I returned to my scooper work— back to one scooper. In desultory fashion, I scooped out rice and dumped it into the bags. I had one eye on my job and one eye on the clock as I muttered to myself, "I can't wait until it's 5:00 and I can get the $%&#!* out of here!"

MORAL OF THE STORY

When I first told this story to managers, I drew three morals of the story:

1. **Employee engagement matters.** When employees approach their jobs with enthusiasm and commitment to the organization's goals, they make a positive impact on the bottom line.

2. **Employee engagement is not fixed.** It goes up or down depending on the environment. Based on conditions in my working environment as a scooper, I went from high engagement to going-through-the-motions low engagement.

3. **Without leadership and accountability, you'll never maximize employee engagement.** After basic instructions, the staff left us alone. There was no management leadership when we needed it. As a result, engagement and productivity plunged.

Although I still think these story morals are accurate, based on subsequent reflection, I added three new ones:

4. **Accountability begins with each individual.** My initial analysis was external. I judged the behavior of the people who walked off the job and the labeler who wouldn't bag rice. I also judged management.

Yet what about me? What might I have done differently? It's easy to look out the window and assess others, but what about looking in the mirror and assessing yourself? It struck me that self-accountability was a critical ingredient of high engagement, and I needed to apply this principle to myself. That's when I realized I could have done more.

5. **Fully engaged relationships share a sense of purpose, something greater than each of us.** We aren't simply following orders or collecting a paycheck, we're making a difference. Presumably all seven of us volunteers shared a sense of purpose and wanted to make a difference, at least in the beginning. Think of the labeler. What did she do during the production slowdown? She stayed productive. Yet when I approached her, I mentioned none of this. I was caught up in my solution. I told her what I wanted without explaining why. I said nothing about how she could help our team, the food bank, and needy families by stepping outside her comfort zone into a new job, an opportunity only made possible because of her initiative in labeling bags in advance. Like most managers, I missed an opportunity to connect the two of us to a shared purpose and opportunity to make a difference that mattered.

6. **In fully engaged workplace relationships, people connect as human beings.** Employees are more than badge numbers, job descriptions, or robots that

can fog mirrors. Yet I didn't know the name of the labeler or any other volunteer. We never introduced ourselves. We received our instructions and went to work. Had I made an investment at the personal level, something as simple as learning and using people's names, perhaps the labeler would have been more inclined to listen to me, and perhaps the vanishing scooper and bagger would have felt more of an obligation to support their fellow human beings at the rice assembly table.

The first set of morals counts: Engagement matters, it's not fixed, and leadership is important. So does the second set of morals: Connect with your employees as human beings. Create a shared sense of purpose with opportunities for your employees to make a difference. And while keeping your window clean to observe others, keep that mirror close at hand, continually asking yourself, "What can I do to create a highly engaged workplace?"

CHAPTER

2

EMPLOYEE SELECTION

THE STUPID SWITCH, PART ONE: HIRING
(Don't Conflate an Applicant's Ability to Get a Job with the Ability to Do It)

I once served as president and board chairman of a nonprofit organization. We needed to hire a full-time executive director. I put together a committee and commenced a nationwide search, winnowing applicants to a group of finalists we planned to fly in for interviews.

The first finalist to visit, Roger, had an impressive resume and a powerhouse personality. He seemed to have the right answer to every question. He made us feel good about our "wonderful volunteer efforts that serve your community so well." He expressed admiration of what we'd "accomplished for such an important and worthy cause."

Personally, Roger stroked my ego with comments such as, "Jathan, I can tell your heart is in this organization. Whoever ends up being executive director will be fortunate to have you as board president."

At one point during his visit, Roger pulled me aside and said:

"You know Jathan, I understand you're beginning 'fly-backs' of finalists. Well I'm at the beginning of 'fly-tos' with other organizations interested in making me their executive director. However, I feel so good about you, your organization and your community that if you feel the same way about me, I'm prepared to end my search now."

I ran this opportunity by the other search committee members. Apparently, they were as impressed with Roger as I was. Excited at what we thought was a historic opportunity and fearful we'd lose Roger to another organization, we decided to make him an offer without interviewing the other finalists.

After I presented Roger with our proposal, he said:

"Jathan, I'm touched by your quick action and confidence in me. However, and I'm almost embarrassed to say this, but the economic terms are less than what I expected. Please understand me. This isn't about money. But based on my knowledge of what other organizations pay, I don't think I can accept this offer and feel responsible to my family. Can you do better?"

I again consulted with my committee. We recrunched numbers and budget projections. I went back to Roger with a revised proposal, which he accepted. Like Rick Blaine in Casablanca, I felt like saying, "Roger, I think this is the beginning of a beautiful friendship."

Wrong!

Shortly after his arrival, Roger made his first executive decision. He had a yellow line painted around the parking space closest to the building. He had a sign put up next to it that read, "Reserved: Executive Director."

Roger's next executive decision was to have his office enlarged. I didn't learn about this project until I observed construction under way. When I questioned him about it, Roger said, "This is necessary. It's beneath the dignity and stature of an executive director of an organization of this magnitude to work in an office that's a glorified broom closet."

Things went downhill from there. Roger effectively rewrote his job description, eliminating duties "that aren't the sorts of things an executive director does; they're for subordinates."

The other organization employees soon began complaining about their new boss. They used words like *self-absorbed*, *aloof*, and *imperious*. One employee quit. Others said they were back in the job market.

Over the next few months, additional issues arose. Finally, we decided to fire Roger. We negotiated a contractual buyout, which wasn't cheap. And we started all over again.

Not one of my better moments as president.

MORAL OF THE STORY

When I tell this story to audiences, I ask them if their "Stupid Switch" has ever been flipped: "Have any of you ever conflated the ability of a candidate to get a job with the candidate's ability to do it?" I typically see lots of hands go up, along with groans and sour looks as if to say, "Gee, Jathan, thanks for reminding me of that 'happy' experience."

Bear in mind that job candidates are looking to sell themselves. Some are quite good at it. They overrepresent their skills, experiences, qualifications, and job fitness. They ingratiate themselves by pushing buttons we like having pushed. What the behavioral economists call confirmation bias kicks in. Subconsciously, we start screening information and interpreting it in ways that confirm our initial impression.

Conversely, there are candidates who are a lot better at doing jobs than selling themselves. They may be overly cautious, humble, shy, or seem uncomfortable. As a result, your initial impression may not be favorable. Confirmation bias kicks in again, only this time to screen and interpret information in ways that confirm in your mind that this candidate is not a good choice.

The problem is compounded by the fact that candidates aren't just trying to sell themselves to us; we're looking to be sold. We've got lots of other pressing things to do with our time besides spend it on hiring. We can't wait to fill the position so we can get back to our regular jobs. This makes us highly susceptible to confirmation bias and to cutting corners, such as failing to conduct thorough due diligence to make sure we don't hire people who overpromise and underdeliver.

So the next time you have a hiring decision to make, place your left thumb just below your left earlobe and press. That's to disconnect your Stupid Switch, Part One.

THE STUPID SWITCH, PART TWO: PROMOTIONS
(Beware the Peter Principle)

Morris worked as a technician for a company that manufactured devices used by military and law enforcement. In a group of 15 technicians, Morris was the only African American.

The company's practice was to promote from within. Management typically selected the best workers for promotion to supervisor.

In terms of productivity, quality, and safety, Morris was an outstanding employee. Jim, the department head, designated him acting supervisor, the first step in the promotion process. This meant that when the regular supervisor, Sandra, was away, Morris became acting supervisor of his group.

At the time of the announcement that Morris would become the acting supervisor, several coworkers congratulated him. However, the good feeling soon changed.

During Morris's first stint as acting supervisor, he interacted with the other technicians in a way that was markedly different from Sandra. Sandra had a low-key, easygoing management style, whereas Morris was more demanding. This contrast resulted in two technicians complaining to Jim about how Morris treated them.

After Sandra's return, Jim sat down with Morris. "While you were acting supervisor, we received complaints about how you were treating employees. Words like *harsh* and *mean* were used."

Morris said, "I wasn't harsh or mean to anyone who did their job. I learned in the military that there's got to be accountability. If people aren't doing their jobs, you've got to let them know in no uncertain terms."

"I agree to a point," Jim said, "but we have a fairly easy-going culture here, and Sandra's style is pretty laid back.

"I'm not saying you should look the other way when employees don't perform, but I think your approach needs to be lower key. Otherwise, the contrast between you and Sandra will be too much for people to accept."

Morris was silent.

Jim continued, "I still think you're a terrific employee and have excellent leadership potential. In fact, I'm prepared to send you to a management-training program at company expense and on company time. It will improve your communication skills and better prepare you for a supervisory position."

Morris replied, "I don't need to take a class! The military taught me what I needed to know about management. If you ask me, the person who needs to take the class is Sandra."

"Thanks for the suggestion," Jim said. "But Sandra's style is more in line with our philosophy and culture. If you want to move into management here Morris, you're going to have to change your approach."

The meeting ended. Morris did not pursue the training opportunity.

A few weeks later, Sandra left for a week's vacation. Despite some misgivings, Jim put Morris in charge. The week did not go well.

Four technicians went to Jim. One was in tears. Another threatened to resign. This employee had been one of those who had congratulated Morris when he'd been designated acting supervisor.

Jim sat down with Morris and heard a familiar response.

"I know what I'm doing," Morris said. "I learned how to manage people in the military. You don't coddle people, that's all."

Jim repeated the offer of management training. Morris again declined.

"Well then Morris, we can't let this continue. You've given me no choice. We're going to select another technician to be acting supervisor."

"I don't think the problem is the way I manage people," Morris said. "I think it may be because white employees aren't used to being supervised by a black man."

"No one brought up race," Jim said.

"I wouldn't expect them to. That doesn't mean it isn't a factor."

Morris subsequently filed a claim of race discrimination with the local antidiscrimination agency and the company retained me as legal counsel to represent it in defending the claim. At a mediation session, my client proposed that if Morris withdrew his claim, they would work with him on a customized management-skills program in which he'd receive training and coaching. It would be designed to enable him to set expectations and hold people accountable in a manner compatible with the company's culture.

Morris turned down the offer. His bitterness remained.

We ended up negotiating a settlement that included his resignation of employment in exchange for severance pay. Despite Morris's having been an excellent technician with a promising future, his career with my client was over.

MORAL OF THE STORY

My client made a mistake other employers frequently make: the Stupid Switch, Part Two, where you conflate the ability of employees to do their current job with their ability to do a different job. My client assumed Morris's success in his hourly technician role would necessarily translate into success in a supervisory position. Yet the former focused on achieving individual goals while the latter focused on achieving group goals. Little or no thought was given to the different perspective, skills, and approach needed when shifting from applying one's own energies and skills to guiding and channeling others' energies and skills.

When the differences between current job and new job are identified upfront with specificity, the selection process, criteria, interview questions, and performance expectations get seen in a new light. The promotion process becomes less a matter of chance, and the likelihood of the Peter Principle (promotion to a level of incompetence) greatly diminishes.

So the next time you have a promotion decision to make, place your right thumb just below your right earlobe and press. That'll disconnect Stupid Switch, Part Two.

Race made this situation more challenging (and is the reason I know the story). However, companies regularly make promotion mistakes regardless of race or other demographic characteristics.

The sad irony here is that the employer earnestly wanted to promote Morris in part because of his race. It wanted to diversify its otherwise white management team and felt Morris would be a great addition. Hence the repeated offers of management-skills development even after he had filed a claim.

On the other hand, it's not shocking that Morris attributed the problem to race. From his perspective, he was doing nothing wrong; the criticism was unmerited and unfair. Like virtually every African American male I have known, Morris had experienced racial discrimination and mistreatment in his past. It's often impossible to scrub your perspective clean of such painful memories.

In my view, the company made a common mistake. It checked the "Affirmative Action Mission Accomplished" box merely by giving Morris the promotion. But it gave no thought to what would be needed to ensure his success in the new position. Although management wanted Morris to succeed, it essentially waited for him to fail. That's when it started the dialogue on leadership expectations. It would have been far better for all parties had management been clear about those expectations before putting Morris in a position to succeed or fail.

BEATING THE COIN TOSS
(To Make Good Employee-Selection Decisions,
Zero in on Core Behaviors)

In my 30-plus-year career, I have employed many administrative assistants. Experience and satisfaction levels have varied widely, from, "Thank goodness she's on my team!" to "OMG! What was I thinking when I hired him?!"

My employee-selection success rate improved dramatically after I started using Star Profiles.

Here's the first one I did. I wrote it when I worked for a law firm, still practicing law while spending increasing time on the road giving presentations. The firm had a four-page job description for legal assistants. However, my Star Profile had just three sentences:

- ▸ Generates and files documents promptly and accurately.
- ▸ Takes charge of my professional and administrative compliance.
- ▸ Puts himself or herself in my travel shoes, making arrangements that consider time, cost, who I need to see, and what needs to happen.

Regarding the first sentence, documents have long constituted my professional lifeblood. Promptness and accuracy are essential. With either compromised, my ability to take care of my clients is compromised.

As for the second sentence, my administrative and professional compliance responsibilities involve many details, especially in my law practice days. Neglect or carelessness could cause major headaches, such as the time a lack of attention to licensing details resulted in my receiving an official court letter informing me that I was practicing law without authorization—a big no-no! Or the time a hit-or-miss approach to processing my expense reports resulted in my being shorted over a year's time of over $3,000. I truly needed an assistant who would take charge of these responsibilities.

The third sentence focused on my increasing travel load. If you've ever had a bad travel experience, you know why I desired an assistant who would figure out what I needed and, with near-fanatical devotion to detail, get me to where I was going and back. Without such support, my professional effectiveness went down while my stress level went up, such as when a company hired me to conduct workshops on three consecutive days in three cities. The cities were essentially in a straight line, with the two outer cities being about a two-and-a-half-hour drive from the middle one. Since I could fly in and out of any of them, the plan was simple: fly into one city, do the workshop, rent a car, drive to the next city, do the second workshop, drive to the third city, do the final workshop, return the car, and fly home from the last city. Simple and straightforward, eh? Unfortunately, my pre-star-profile assistant scheduled me to start in the middle city. This meant that after the first workshop, I drove two-and-a-half hours to the next city. However, after the second day's workshop, I had to drive five hours to the last one.

Experiences like this inspired me to create my first Star Profile and use it in the hiring process. My approach has been simple. Share the profile characteristics with the candidates and get their views. In some cases, candidates have said, "If that's what you really need, I'm not the right person for this job." I ask you: What better time to find this out than before you hire them?

If the candidate says, "That speaks to me," I ask for a specific experience of his or hers that would help me predict we will see the profile behavior in the future. If one is offered, I'll say something like, "You know, perceptions differ from one person to another. To make really sure, I may need you to get contact information for people who have knowledge of the experience you share so that I can ask them for their perception as well."

This step has proved highly effective in separating candidates good at getting but not doing jobs from candidates good at doing but not getting jobs. The smooth confidence of the former quickly fades, while the discomfort of the latter likewise fades. With the former, I sometimes have had to suppress a smile at their sudden tongue-tiedness. "It's okay, take your time," I'll say. "If you can't think of anything, you can't think of anything." With the latter, they often express their own interest in finding out what others perceive and go out of their way to get me contact information.

I won't say my new approach raised my hiring odds to perfection. However, they have soared past the 50–50 mark that prevailed before. Moreover, having the Star Profile conversation during the hiring process has made their transition to actual employment much easier and more effective.

I've put away my coin.

MORAL OF THE STORY

If done properly, Star Profiles possess few words but create powerful, action-oriented pictures of what's most important in a particular job from the perspective of the person to whom that position reports. In the case above, there were many other things legal assistants did. After all, there was the firm's four-page job description. For me, however, success or failure centered on those three sentences.

Although short and to the point, Star Profiles don't necessarily come together quickly. The most effective ones get honed and crafted to accurately depict the core of job success. Every word counts. Some managers have spent hours zeroing in on and fine-tuning the words that best capture the actions that matter most. Nevertheless, when you think about how much time and effort managers expend, and how much stress they suffer, because of bad hiring decisions that are revealed by performance and disciplinary problems, the investment is small in relation to the return.

Thus, I recommend that you likewise make the investment and put away your coin.

THE PROFESSOR HAS A CLOSE CALL
(Use a Star Profile to Avoid Premature
Decision Making)

Maria was the director of a small Latino Studies Department at a Midwestern university. Until recently, the university had been able to afford only one full-time, tenure-track position—hers.

Things changed after a wealthy donor agreed to fund another position in Latino studies. This meant Maria would finally have a colleague, her very own associate director ("I can delegate!")

With eagerness, Maria jumped into the university process for hiring a professor. She formed a search committee and began looking for a fellow scholar to join her.

During the search process, Maria and I had a conversation about Star Profiles and how they're used to make hiring decisions. Maria expressed interest in learning more, but time, distance, and other obligations prevented it from happening.

Several months later, Maria called me to say that the search committee had narrowed the finalists to five and were about to fly the first one in for interviews, faculty meetings, and a guest lecture. Maria was very excited but also nervous. A good choice would be heaven, but a bad one—given the procedural hassle of terminating a professor—would be hell.

I offered to give her a crash course on the Star Profile concept. She eagerly accepted.

As a result, Maria came up with four sentences that captured the core behaviors of a star associate director:

► Provides teaching that attracts students to our program.
► Produces tenure-worthy scholarship.
► Interacts with members of the community to promote interest in and support for our program.
► Collaborates with and supports the director in furthering the program's goals.

Maria explained her four sentences:

"As for the first characteristic, we are a fairly new program. It will be critical to have the kind of teacher who makes students want to attend our courses and get the word out to other students.

"As for the second sentence, I'm not looking for an academic superstar. In fact, an academic superstar would probably spend too much time on scholarly work and want to leave once he or she got an offer from a more prestigious university. On the other hand, this person has to produce work of sufficient quality to get tenure. Otherwise, I'll have a major problem in the future.

"As for the third sentence, we don't have a lot of money and depend on outside support. I need an associate director who interacts well with people who aren't fellow scholars but who can help us.

"As for the fourth, I'm going to have to work with this person extremely closely. Trust has to be absolute. I need a colleague I can collaborate with and who also has my back."

A day after Maria finished her Star Profile, the first finalist arrived—Joseph, a candidate from an eastern university who had already established a reputation as an up-and-coming scholar. His curriculum vitae was very impressive, probably the most impressive of the five finalists.

Joseph's guest lecture was a smashing success. It dripped with brilliance and authoritative elocution.

That evening, Maria hosted a reception for Joseph at her home. Fellow faculty members as well as program donors and community supporters wandered through her kitchen, dining area, and living room with plates of food.

After a while, Maria couldn't help but notice that Joseph had been locked in a circle with three professors in an animated discussion. They seemed oblivious to everyone else.

She pulled out of her pocket the note on which she'd written the Star Profile and thought, "Hmmm, I don't doubt characteristics one and two, Joseph's ability to teach effectively and produce tenure-worthy scholarship. But interacting with members of the community to support the program, I'm not so sure."

Maria decided to try a little experiment. She tapped Joseph on the shoulder and said, "Excuse me, Joseph, may I speak with you for a minute?"

Joseph stepped out of the circle and faced her. "If you don't mind," she said, "before people start leaving, I'd like to introduce you. And if you'd care to say a few words, that would be great."

"I have not prepared remarks for this occasion," Joseph said.

"That's fine," Maria said. "You don't have to say anything substantial, just maybe a greeting and an impromptu word or two."

With a serious tone, Joseph said, "I don't do impromptu."

"Okay," said Maria, "but I'm going to introduce you anyway." With that, she tapped her glass with a spoon, getting everyone's attention.

"Hi everyone. Thank you so much for coming out this evening to meet Joseph. I hope you had an opportunity to hear his wonderful lecture earlier today. And I want to thank Joseph for traveling here to join us this day."

With that, Maria stopped speaking and looked at Joseph. All eyes were on him. Joseph looked around the room but said nothing. An awkward silence followed. The silence was broken when Joseph turned to the professors with whom he'd been engaged earlier and plunged back into conversation with them. He remained thus engaged until nearly all of the other guests had left.

Subsequently, Maria called me. She explained what had happened and said:

"Oh my goodness! When I think how close the search committee and I were to offering Joseph the position, I shudder. What a nightmare that would have been! 'Interacts with members of the community to promote interest in and support for our program'—I don't think so! 'Collaborates with and supports the director'—I definitely don't think so! All I can say is, 'Whew!'"

Maria and her committee ultimately hired another finalist, with Maria using the Star Profile as a discussion point and assessment tool. Maria found her long-term "star," who eventually succeeded her as program director.

As for Joseph, about a year after this episode, Maria attended an academic conference and met an attendee from a university that had hired Joseph. The attendee told Maria, "We were all excited at first. The guy is brilliant. But, off the record, he's an arrogant jerk!"

Maria smiled understandingly and nodded sympathetically.

MORAL OF THE STORY

If you're contemplating an important decision with long-term consequences, it pays to invest in the decision-making process. Maria was about to plunge off a cliff similar to the one I plunged off of in "Stupid Switch, Part One." Instead, she saved herself by creating and using a Star Profile.

By projecting into the future a moving picture of what would constitute success, and then zooming in on the necessary behavioral characteristics, Maria was able to make a wise choice. She saw that academic scholarship was not the be-all-and-end-all that she and other faculty members tended to assume. Other characteristics, ones less obvious or tangible, were equally if not more important, such as how this associate director would work with Maria as director and how the person would connect with members of the community. By moving from "Who has the most impressive qualifications?" to "Who possesses the behavioral traits most likely to produce the results we need?," Maria dramatically upped the odds of a good, long-term selection decision.

THE SUCCESSION SCRAMBLE SINKS
(Succession Planning Should Not Be Left
to Chance)

When I served as president and board chairman of a nonprofit organization, I didn't think about succession until my term was nearing the end and the deadline approached for nominating a successor.

I began a succession scramble. I asked one board member I liked and respected if she would consider succeeding me as president and board chair. "Not enough time for the job," she said. I asked another board member—similar response. I began to get nervous. I tried a third. Another rejection!

Getting desperate, I asked a board member who I was confident would say yes. Smart and hard working, Richard was also ambitious—and rather abrasive. From time to time, employees and board members had been on the receiving end of his blunt observations.

Although somewhat skeptical, the board accepted my recommendation that Richard succeed me. The members voted in favor, and Richard soon took over.

Almost from day one, Richard's different leadership style surfaced. Instead of engaging in collaborative decision making, he administered strong doses of old-school command and control. This caused friction. Relieved to have passed the reins, however, I kept my head down and resisted urgings to intervene, including declining requests that I resume my former position.

Tensions worsened. Recrimination and conflict became the norm. After several rounds of verbal fisticuffs with the board, Richard resigned under pressure and in anger. The whole episode was fraught with pain, lost opportunity, and harm to our organization's mission.

Not exactly the best way to leave a legacy.

MORAL OF THE STORY

In hindsight, I realized that as leader, I committed several mistakes. First, I waited too long to focus on succession planning. It should have been part of my thinking from the beginning of my term, not the end. Second, I spent insufficient time reflecting on my organization's strengths, weaknesses, opportunities, and threats (SWOT), and on what behavioral traits would be most important in a successor. Instead, I focused on my need: getting the succession monkey off of my back. Third, after the change occurred, happy to be unburdened, I became passive and did not help set the stage for my successor. It was, "Here's the baton. Run!"

Having subsequently used Star Profiles in succession planning and having coached others to do so, I can say they're positive difference makers. Had I applied this approach then, the profile would have said something like this:

PRESIDENT/BOARD CHAIR

- Combines humility and drive in working with the board and staff to further our mission.

- Energetically drums up financial and other support from members and donors.

- Promotes teamwork throughout the organization, from volunteers to staff to the board to the community members we serve.

- Helps keep our financial house in order.

In addition to disconnecting my Stupid Switch, a Star Profile would have been a useful recruitment tool. Before I approached Richard in desperation, I would have had very different conversations with the board members I attempted to recruit. The focus would not have been their fulfilling an obligation or relieving my burden. It would have been a discussion of needed leadership behavior and why their past behavior indicated a good fit for the future. At a minimum, I predict they'd have had a tougher time telling me no and would have helped me recruit someone else.

Moreover, the profile would have been useful after the new leader took over. It would have provided a basis for an ongoing dialogue between current president, past president, board, and staff about what really matters.

Great leaders care about the legacies they leave. That legacy is more than the results you produce while in the job. It includes what you did to ensure that your organization was in good hands after you left. Treat succession as a critical responsibility and use a Star Profile to help. You'll leave a legacy worth leaving.

CHAPTER
3

PERFORMANCE MANAGEMENT

PUNCHED BY THE CEO—YOU CAN'T BE SERIOUS! (A Strong Organizational Culture Can Overcome a Leader's Occasional Boneheaded Moves)

Carl should have been an employment lawyer's dream.

President and CEO of an electronics company that had grown to nearly 1,500 employees, Carl occasionally used some unorthodox approaches in employee relations.

The company received notice of a harassment claim from a former saleswoman, Trisha, who alleged that "the President and CEO of the company harassed me with repeated questions, comments, and statements about my sexual orientation and practices with my female partner. In addition, he touched me in unwelcomed and unwanted ways, including striking me with his fist."

I asked Carl about the allegations. "Surely they're made up, right?"

"Nope," Carl said, "They're essentially true."

Uh oh!

I figured we would be in for a long and expensive haul in the legal system. However, it didn't work out that way. The claim soon went away. No money changed hands. Trisha dropped it.

It turned out that Trisha wasn't really upset with Carl for this behavior. The two had carried on a running discussion/debate about heterosexual versus homosexual sex. Workplace appropriate? Heck no! But it was something they did. In fact, Trisha's female partner had been introduced to her by Carl.

What about the physical abuse? On one occasion at work, while joking around, Carl punched Trisha in the arm. Trisha, a former college athlete, responded by punching Carl in the stomach, causing him to double over, knees sinking to the floor. By all accounts, Trisha felt she had taken appropriate remedial action. Indeed, coworkers praised her self-help efforts.

For his part, Carl bore her no grudge. After his breath returned, he said, "Nice punch."

So why did Trisha bring this claim? It turns out she'd recently left the company after receiving a lucrative offer from a competitor. Carl had sent her a letter reminding her of the noncompete agreement she had signed and expressed his willingness to sue her if she violated it. Adopting the stance that the best defense is a good offense, Trisha responded with the harassment claim, which she hoped would give her leverage in narrowing the scope of her postemployment competitive restrictions.

Carl wouldn't budge, however. Trisha needed to comply with the noncompete agreement as written or the company would sue, regardless of any harassment claim she might assert. Once Trisha realized Carl was serious, she asked for her job back. Carl agreed, and that's the last I heard about this particular employee.

Case closed.

MORAL OF THE STORY

First of all, the moral of this story is *not* to joke with your employees about sex, much less punch them.

This moral has to do with my overall experience with Carl's company. Given the company's large size, presence in some highly litigious states, and Carl's, shall we say, unorthodox leadership style, you might think I landed in lawyer billable-hour heaven. Yet I never once went to court on the company's behalf. Employees didn't sue, even after being fired. I also noticed that the company had grown substantially over the years and had done extraordinarily well financially, outperforming its competitors.

What was the reason for this combination of low litigiousness and high profitability? As Carl explained, shortly after taking over as CEO, he implemented a practice by which every new hire would be scrutinized closely for long-term fit. Supervisors were trained to evaluate new employees on their ability to meet the company's high performance/high accountability expectations. If there were signs of a potential nonfit, supervisors were required to work more closely with the new employee with a view to managing that person up or out at the earliest opportunity.

After this initial review period, which was not expected to be longer than two months, if an employee subsequently had problems meeting expectations, scrutiny would fall first on the supervisor. Were there warning signs during the initial review period that the supervisor overlooked or chose to ignore? If so, the question became whether that supervisor should still be supervising.

Carl explained:

"We fired lots of people over the years, but we were always clear to everyone that high performance was nonnegotiable. Most employee terminations occurred early in their employment. Usually they weren't surprised and didn't feel it was unfair.

"For employees who had been here a while but whose performance had dropped, we'd give them a chance to correct things but didn't wait forever. It was strictly business; nothing personal. Also, we didn't tolerate managers who let employee performance slide. It was, 'Fix the problem one way or the other.'"

One might think that such an environment created low morale. Yet the opposite was true. Carl had given employees a stake in the company's profits, which helped. However, perhaps of even greater effect was the contagious attitude of employees who saw themselves as high performers in a high-performance environment. Carl's company preached and practiced the philosophy that accountability for high performance starts with management to create an environment where employees can excel. This included proactively pruning from the workforce employees and managers who didn't fit the culture.

The performance-management lesson is this: Set the expectations bar early and clearly. Make sure all managers and supervisors consistently hew to it in their dealings with their employees. Accountability starts with the boss.

THE NEW CADILLAC, THE FUR COAT, AND THE CONFIDENTIALITY CLAUSE
(Beware the Law of Employee Speculation)

In the mid-1980s, a company in the energy industry hired me to conduct a workplace investigation and report my findings to its board of directors. As a young lawyer, this was a first for me. I was excited.

Karen, an engineering assistant, had complained to human resources that she was the victim of gender-based pay discrimination and that her boss, George, the head of the engineering department, had retaliated against her.

During my investigation, I uncovered evidence validating Karen's claims. She had been working for the past two years as an engineering assistant earning $30,000 per year (in 1985 dollars). Yet she performed work identical to that of four male employees, each of whom had the title engineer and earned $45,000 per annum.

George, who was known behind his back as Mr. Old School, explained during our interview that the pay disparity was "entirely justified." "Look," he said, "we're paying her more than what she got at her previous job. Besides, those guys have families to support."

("Old School" should have been "Old, Old School")

Karen alleged that before going to human resources, she had raised the pay issue with George, but he had not responded well. "George told me that if I knew what was good for me, I would keep my mouth shut. Two days after this conversation, he told me he had changed his mind about approving me for a professional certification program. He said he only did such things for 'team players.'"

In my interview, George denied retaliating against Karen. However, his denial didn't help his credibility. "That little lady should be happy to have the job she's got," he said.

(Let's make that "Old, Old, Old School")

At a meeting with the board of directors to discuss my findings, a consensus quickly emerged on the path forward. Step 1: Fire George. In addition to his treatment of Karen, other information surfaced about George's managerial practices, bringing to mind a 1950s science fiction movie starring James Arness of later *Gunsmoke* fame. Arness plays a creature from outer space who crash lands in the North Pole and becomes entombed in a block of ice until discovered centuries later. After the ice melts . . .

Step 2 was settling Karen's claim. In exchange for a full release of claims, I negotiated the following deal: (a) The company "promoted" her to the engineering position she'd been doing for two years, (b) it increased her salary to the same rate paid her male coworkers, and (c) it provided a lump-sum payment of $15,000 in recognition of past lost income.

As I explained to the board of directors, under applicable law, $15,000 represented a mere one-fourth of the double-damages lost-pay award Karen would likely receive if she sued, not to mention the other economic damages she'd likely receive. After hearing this, a board member said, "Let's get this done! Heck, I'll write the check myself!"

Under the circumstances, I had negotiated a terrific deal for my client and basked in the glow. "Thump, thump, thump," went my ego. Unfortunately, however, a large dose of humility awaited me.

As is typical in settlement agreements, the one I drafted included a provision barring Karen from disclosing terms of the deal. Other employees were aware of her claim and that it had been resolved but didn't know the details.

To the best of my knowledge, Karen kept her end of the bargain. However, soon after the deal was cut, she arrived at work in a brand new, fully loaded Cadillac. On a chilly winter morning, she stepped out of her new car in a new coat that extended from neck to ankles and for which many small furry creatures had probably given up their lives.

Coworkers rushed up to Karen. "What did the company give you?!" they cried. "Tell us!"

Karen dutifully replied, "I'm sorry but the company's lawyer made me sign a paper that says I can't tell you."

Word of Karen's "deal" spread like wildfire.

Over the next two years, I had the opportunity to learn what kind of speculation had gone on concerning how much money Karen supposedly received. The rumor mill had a high range—$600,000. (Mind you, we're talking 1985 dollars.) It had a low range—a scant $300,000. That's right, the lowest any employee thought Karen received to settle her claims was 20 times the actual amount.

How did I learn this information? Because over those next two years, I had to wade through nearly 40 new claims of employment discrimination filed by Karen's coworkers.

MORAL OF THE STORY

When employees don't know, they speculate. And for employers, their speculation is always worse than reality. I call this the Law of Employee Speculation, which arises whenever management fails to share information employees consider important. They fill in the blank with speculation. If management withholds good news, employees will assume it's negative or at best neutral. If the news would be neutral, it will be assumed bad. If bad, it will be assumed catastrophic.

Setting aside the legal system for a moment, every management or organizational guru I've studied has criticized American management for doing a lousy job at sharing information with employees. Why is the problem so prevalent? Most managers intuitively tend to hold their cards close to the chest out of fear that too much employee knowledge could be dangerous. Yet this fear becomes self-fulfilling. Employees not only fill in the blank with something worse than what the manager is fearful to disclose, their trust and respect in management erodes.

Accordingly, when it comes to information that may be relevant to an employee's job status or sense of well-being or belonging in the organization, the question should not be "Why share?" but "Why not share?" The presumption should be to share, not the other way around. This rule applies not only when the news is good but when it's bad, sometimes especially when it's bad.

Are there exceptions? Can the presumption be rebutted? Sure. If you work for Coca-Cola, I wouldn't recommend you post the secret recipe on the Internet. Indeed, my subsequent settlement agreements often still included confidentiality provisions. However, that didn't prevent me from occasionally wishing, such as in Karen's case, that company management had "accidentally" left a copy of the agreement in the employee break room. A half hour's availability would have sufficed.

"TEXAS WES" AND THE SAME DAY SUMMARY
(A Documentation Tool That Actually Works)

Perhaps the most frustrating subject I've taught managers is documentation. Why? Because for the longest time, no one ever practiced what I preached.

"Texas Wes" is a good example. COO of a large oil and gas company, Wes attended one of my management training programs a number of years ago. A few months later, he called me to review a personnel issue: He intended to fire one of his employees based on unsatisfactory performance. Because the employee was turning 60 and had been with the company a long time, Wes had concerns about a potential age-discrimination claim. He wanted to make sure he had his ducks in a row.

"Jay-uh-thon," Wes began in his Texas drawl, "you'll be proud of me. I followed all of your teachin's. I was direct and specific about performance problems and about the consequences if he didn't fix them. No surprises here!"

"Great, Wes," I replied, "I'm glad to hear it. Send me the documents. I'll take a look and call you back with what no doubt will be a thumbs-up. Just send me the documents."

There was silence on Wes's end of the phone.

"Wes?" I said, "Are you still there?"

More silence.

"Wes? . . . Wes?"

Finally: "Aw hell, Jay-uh-thon. Ah hate to write! I don't have time for that %#$@&*!"

Needless to say, without a scrap of supporting documentation, Wes didn't get my thumbs-up for a performance-based termination of a long-time employee turning 60.

Experiences like this forced me back to the drawing board. My wonderful documentation tools with all their well-crafted bells and whistles weren't getting the job done. How come? Because they weren't user friendly.

I thought about what might be a simple and easy enough tool that a busy manager would use and would still add value. And I thought. And thought.

Finally, it struck me: I could teach managers how to write opposing counsel confirmation letters. While you scratch your head, let me explain.

I hope this doesn't shock you too much, but I learned early in my law career that not all lawyers can be trusted. (I'll give you a moment to collect yourself.) For example, I'd have a telephone conversation with opposing counsel, reach an understanding about what would happen next, only to discover later that the other attorney didn't deliver when the time came. When confronted, however, opposing counsel invariably denied our understanding, often counterclaiming that I had agreed to something I hadn't.

To combat this problem, I developed a practice of sending short, to-the-point confirming letters after each conversation of significance. The letter would begin, "Dear Lawyer Representing the Forces of Evil." (Actually I wasn't quite that snarky. Not quite.)

The body of the letter would begin with something like, "This letter summarizes our conversation this morning regarding . . ." I would then summarize the key points, particularly the things that had been agreed to going forward. The letter would close with a statement like, "If I haven't summarized our conversation accurately, please let me know immediately."

This practice became a game changer for me in dealing with opposing attorneys. So I thought it might be a game changer for managers as well.

And sure enough, it has been.

MORAL OF THE STORY

Calling the tool the Opposing Counsel Confirmation Letter probably won't work for you. Instead, I suggest calling it the Same Day Summary. The Same Day Summary follows a conversation you've had with an employee that you consider significant. Here are the elements:

► The document summarizes only the key points actually spoken by you or the employee. You're not taking meeting minutes.

► It's prepared and given to the employee within a day (24 hours) of the discussion. Given how quickly memories fade, the sooner the better.

► It's no more than a page. Most Same Day Summaries are shorter than a page, often just a brief paragraph with a few bullet points.

► Instead of requiring a signature, confirmation, or agreement with the substance of the discussion, the Same Day Summary asks only that you be promptly informed if the recipient disagrees with the accuracy of the summary.

► In most instances, email works fine. It gives you date, time, and tracking information and can easily be stored.

► No lengthy treatises. No creative writing. No racking your memory. No arguments or debates. And no having to track down your employee for a response.

This tool is so easy to use yet so effective that a great many managers (not to mention numerous human resources professionals) have made it part of their communications toolkit. In fact, a certain executive from the Lone Star State now not only uses Same Day Summaries himself, but if you're a manager who reports to him, you'd best be using them with your employees as well. Otherwise, you're in for a real talk'n' to!

BONUS MORAL OF THE STORY

Shortly after I began teaching this tool, I flew to Fresno, California, to speak to a group of managers and human resources professionals. During the Q&A afterward, a veteran of labor and employment law warfare in the Golden State posed a challenge: "Mr. Janove, doesn't your Same Day Summary create excessive risks for employers, at least in our jurisdiction, the People's Republic of California?"

She elaborated: "If we need to rely on a Same Day Summary to show that an employee received progressive discipline, won't the employee be able to say he never got it? And we'll be in trouble because we can't prove otherwise since there's no signature requirement."

I replied, "You're absolutely right. The Same Day Summary does create that risk. And it must sound kind of nutty hearing it preached by a lawyer who's supposed to keep employers out of court.

"However, your risk analysis needs to go deeper. What happens when you require managers to obtain signatures on documents describing employee performance, attendance, or behavior issues? In my experience, usually it doesn't happen, or you wish it hadn't. In my view, the risk that your managers won't write such documents properly or timely is even greater."

I took another step up on the soapbox. "In addition," I said, "requiring signatures tends to make supervisor-employee relations adversarial. Sometimes employees refuse to sign, which makes the document an even bigger pain in the neck, or they write something inflammatory in the margin such as, 'As an older worker, I'm being victimized,' which of course causes a new set of troubles. That is why I often find documentation of employee problems less helpful to the employer than to the employee suing the employer."

Building up a head of steam, I took another step: "With Same Day Summaries, you avoid these problems. You don't have to wrestle with an employee over his signature. You can explain that the document isn't meant to punish but to give the employee the best chance to succeed by keeping everyone on the same page. It creates a 'no surprises' relationship. How many employees will object to that?"

Teetering a bit at the height, I took another step: "If you make Same Day Summaries a regular practice, not just for problems but for discussions about opportunities, policy changes, new game plans, successes, and positive employee behavior, they won't associate them with trouble or speculate about the motives that underlie them. Plus, if you incorporate them in your document-retention system, you can reduce the 'I never got this document' risk almost to nil."

I added: "I'm not saying you would never require a signature from an employee, such as with a final disciplinary warning. But I'll make this prediction: If you make the Same Day Summary a regular practice, chances are you'll never have to give someone a final disciplinary warning. Why? Because problematic employee behavior will already have been managed up or managed out. And without your needing an employment lawyer to defend you."

With that, I leaped from my soapbox, headed to the door, and flew home from Fresno with neither feather nor tar.

A FLOOD IN THE LOBBY
(Remote Management Presents Challenges)

Cassandra managed a California resort property. She reported to the regional vice president, Joan, who worked at headquarters in New York.

Cassandra felt that the lobby at her property was dingy, not befitting their clientele. She called Joan.

"I'd like to get the lobby remodeled," Cassandra said. "Would you approve it?"

Joan responded, "Sorry, there isn't money in the budget right now, and revenue is a bit slow, so I'm afraid the answer's no."

After a pause, Joan added with a chuckle, "Of course, we could get lucky. An accident could happen. Then the insurance company would have to pay for it. Ha! Ha!"

About two months later, a hose at the property was left running overnight. It happened to be pointed toward the lobby. By early the next morning, eight inches of water engulfed the lobby.

Cassandra had closed up the property the prior night.

The insurance company paid for the damage and cost of remodeling. However, the insurer's suspicions had been raised. It sent one of its investigators to visit the site. It didn't take long to find evidence incriminating Cassandra.

When confronted, she confessed to flooding the lobby. However, she invoked the so-called Nuremberg defense. She said, "It's not my fault. I was only following my boss's orders."

When informed of Cassandra's explanation, Joan was aghast. "I can't believe she's saying that! I was joking. That's insane! No one in their right mind would have thought I was serious, that I would order an employee to commit a fraudulent, illegal act!"

The insurance company and her employer believed Joan. Nevertheless, her company had to repay all of the insurance proceeds plus interest, costs related to the investigation, and some attorneys' fees. This made for an extremely expensive lobby remodeling job.

Not surprisingly, the company fired Cassandra. She responded by hiring an attorney who sent a written demand that she be reinstated with full back pay or be compensated with substantial economic damages "as a victim of wrongful discharge."

The company's response was short and to the point: "Walk away from us and we'll walk away from you. Sue us, and we'll sue you for every dollar this disaster cost us."

Undeterred, Cassandra proceeded. After protracted litigation, the court dismissed her claims against the company. On the company's countersuit against her, the court awarded full damages.

Following Cassandra's unsuccessful appeal, the judgment against her exceeded $100,000. Having already taken out a second mortgage and extended her credit cards to pay for litigation costs and her attorneys' fees, Cassandra ended up in bankruptcy. She had lost her job, career, and savings. For her, the lobby remodeling job was very expensive indeed.

One moral of the story is that sometimes humor is no joking matter. When was the last time you said defensively, "I was only joking"? Or someone said that to you? This case illustrates the danger of misconstrued humor, especially when there's a difference in authority level. People in subordinate positions often don't ask a clarifying question from fear the boss will get annoyed and think they're dense. The miscommunication risk goes up.

On another level, this story points out the challenges of remote management. With Joan in New York and Cassandra in California, the potential for miscommunication increased dramatically. There weren't the quick check-ins or other ways people keep on the same page when they work near each other.

Without being in the presence of the person with whom you're communicating, you can't detect visual or auditory clues that your message is coming across in ways you don't intend. The misunderstanding continues without awareness or opportunity to clarify.

The Same Day Summary tool described in "Texas Wes" is especially useful for managers who supervise others remotely. Following that telephone or other real-time conversation, send a quick email summary of key points to the other person. In Joan's case, a simple "As I mentioned, we're not able to remodel the lobby at this time" would probably have sufficed.

Managers who manage remote employees have found Same Day Summaries to be highly useful. And to the best of my knowledge, none of them have had floods in their lobbies.

PERFORMANCE REVIEW FOLLIES
(Real-Time Feedback Beats Surprise Feedback)

There was a knock at my office door. I opened it and saw my law firm's managing partner, William, standing with two other partners.

"Jathan," he said, "the Associate Review Committee has finished your review and would like to discuss it with you. Is now a good time?"

With a lump in my throat and palms turning moist, I said, "Uh, sure. Come on in."

My firm conducted annual performance reviews for associate attorneys. In December, a committee of three partners led by the managing partner would interview their fellow partners, soliciting performance feedback about the associates. After the interviews, the committee would compile the feedback and present it to each associate. The stakes were high. They included the associate's bonus for the year, if any; his or her raise for the following year, if any; and the associate's future in the firm—if any.

Even when the review was favorable, the experience was not much fun. It was like being told by your dentist, "Now that was an easy root canal." Of course, when the review wasn't good, the experience could be excruciating.

After shutting my office door, William and the other two partners pulled up chairs around my desk. "Your review is mixed," William said. "Although several partners spoke quite highly of you, you did receive some criticism. In fact, one partner was so disappointed in the quality of your writing he recommends that you be required to take a remedial class on how to write."

That comment stung me like a wasp. I began to turn pale. "Who said I need to take a remedial writing class?" I asked.

William arched an eyebrow at me suspiciously. "Why do you ask?"

"So that I can speak with him to get a better idea of what I need to do to correct my apparent deficiencies." I tried to say this as humbly as possible, but the flush in my cheeks and quiver in my voice may have betrayed the anger I was trying to suppress.

William replied hesitantly, "I suppose sharing that information would be appropriate if used for constructive purposes. It's Samuel."

The rest of the meeting went by in a blur. Only one piece of information stuck. I needed to take a remedial writing class. Me—a practicing attorney, college honors graduate in English with a concentration in journalism, Phi Beta Kappa, columnist for a local newspaper, and someone who's loved to write ever since first grade when my teacher, Mrs. Parker, told my parents, "Jay is a gifted writer."

And I learn this wonderful confidence-building piece of information during my annual performance review. Aaargghh!

The next day, I walked into Samuel's office. Steeling myself, I said as smoothly and evenly as I could, "The Associate Review Committee mentioned that you had concerns about the quality of my writing. I'm wondering if you could elaborate."

Samuel frowned and began to fidget. "I assume you're talking about that assignment I gave you several months ago," he said. "I don't remember it well. But I recall that your memo was hard to get through, and wasn't that helpful."

I attempted to elicit more details, but without success. Although I professed a desire for self-improvement and did my best to conceal my frustration, I seemed to make Samuel increasingly uncomfortable. Finally I said, "Thanks for the info. I'll work on improving my writing skills," and left his office.

However, I wasn't ready to give up. I went to a senior associate who worked a lot with Samuel. "Chris," I said, "can you show me an example of a memo that Samuel likes?"

Chris rummaged through a few files and produced a research memorandum. At a glance, I could see the difference between my writing and this memo. To me, the latter looked like a glorified outline: lots of headings and subheadings with not much text in between.

By contrast, my writing style had been influenced by writers like Marcel Proust and William Faulkner—authors who can go on for pages without a sentence ending. Samuel had a legitimate point. For legal writing at least, his preferred model probably beats the Proustian or Faulknerian one. (Perhaps that's why they're called legal "briefs.")

A few weeks later, I again stepped into Samuel's office. "I've been working hard on improving my writing," I said, lifting the corners of my mouth to project a smile. "I'd like an opportunity to show you the progress I've made. Is there a project I can do for you?"

Samuel seemed pleased with my show of humility and smiled back. He thought for a moment and said, "I have a case with a statute of limitations question. Why don't you research it and write up a memo for me?"

"Great," I said.

After I completed the research and began the memo, I used the outline method from the example Chris showed me. Indeed, I laid it on thick. Practically a sentence didn't go by without another category being started. I broke the memo down into so many subparts, I had to learn new outline symbols. You might say instead of writing the memo vertically down the page, I wrote it horizontally across the page.

After I handed the memo to Samuel, I began to worry a bit. I thought, "What if he thinks I'm being a smart aleck?" (Which, of course, would have been entirely untrue.)

No need to worry, however. Samuel loved the memo. In fact, from that point forward and lasting years later, even after I became a partner in the firm, Samuel was my number one source of work, giving me more projects to do than he gave any other attorney.

Talk about a turnaround.

If you were William, you might defend the performance review process and say something to me like, "You see, Jathan, your experience shows that our system worked. You received pertinent performance feedback, took the initiative, made the necessary corrections, and benefited from all that. A veritable success story."

Don't buy it. I didn't go to Samuel as part of a self-improvement quest. I was mad! I wanted to show him he was wrong and Mrs. Parker was right. My bruised ego motivated me to go to the extraordinary lengths I had to go to overcome Samuel's generalized and stale feedback and find out what I needed.

In my experience, employees receiving performance review criticism as I did are more likely to become discouraged or embittered. Relationships that might have been successful end badly—as my relationship with Samuel had ended temporarily and potentially permanently. After my first assignment, Samuel had ceased giving me work. He'd written me off for future assignments without telling me. It was through the slimmest of chances that we reconnected and a long-term mutually beneficial relationship unfolded.

What if after reading my first memo and being disappointed, Samuel had sat down with me while the problem was fresh in his mind? What if he'd shown me an example of a research memorandum that was written in a manner that met his needs? In December, the Associate Review

Committee might have said this instead: "Samuel told us that last March he gave you an assignment but wasn't happy with the writing. However, he said you subsequently corrected the issue, and he now has full confidence in your work."

Better yet, why not start the clock even sooner? What if when giving me my first assignment, Samuel had discussed his expectations and showed me an example of something he liked? Had he done so, there most likely wouldn't have been a problem in the first place.

In your experience, how many Samuel and Jathan relationships fail not because of an inherent lack of fit but because of a failure to communicate? If your experience is at all like mine, the answer is, "Far too many."

For your reference, here's my list of performance review don'ts and dos:

The Don'ts

- ▶ **Rational lies.** Too often managers rationalize or tell themselves "rational lies" that although honesty is the best policy, the performance review is an exception. It should never be.

- ▶ **Gunnysack feedback.** These managers save up feedback like farmers slowly filling a gunnysack with potatoes—only to drop them over the employee's head at performance review time. Not exactly a bonding moment.

- ▶ **Report card.** Like school teachers at the end of the term, these managers give feedback looking entirely backward, underscoring their superiority and the employee's inferiority.

- ▶ **Creative writing.** The performance review is not a time to exercise your writing skills (such as the manager who wrote, "Maybe you're getting too old for this job.")

- ▶ **Disciplinary tool.** "Needs improvement" is not the same as "Last-chance warning." If you have a disciplinary problem, deal with it directly. Don't use the performance review to tiptoe around it.

As Stephen R. Covey said, begin with the end in mind. Start by thinking of the outcome. What would you like to see in the future that the performance review can help make happen? Take a look in the rearview mirror, but keep your main focus on the road ahead.

The Dos

- ▶ **Behavior that matters.** Avoid the plethora of categories and subcategories. As with Star Profiles, zero in on what really matters and concentrate your feedback there.

- ▶ **Process, not event.** Here's a simple rule: Create a surprise-free zone. A performance review should summarize prior feedback given in real-time.

▸ **Participation of all managers.** All managers should commit to using the performance review process to help their employees succeed. Otherwise they shouldn't be managing.

▸ **Two-way feedback**. The discussion should be two-way—the manager gives and *receives* feedback. What can the manager and employee each do to help them succeed together? The Triple Two technique from "I'll Do It with Anybody but Monique!" (see chapter 6) comes in handy here.

The performance review can be a useful performance management tool. Just avoid the don'ts and practice the dos.

COURSE CORRECTION OR CORRECTIVE ACTION? (When an Employee Falls Short of Expectations, Respond with Curiosity, Not Faultfinding)

The plaintiff's lawyer sent a letter to my client claiming that it had wrongfully discharged his client, a former employee, and demanding $200,000 within 10 days; otherwise, he would file a lawsuit seeking a vastly greater sum.

After my client forwarded the letter to me, I called opposing counsel. I told him that if he held off filing the complaint, I'd investigate the claim and determine whether settlement discussions made sense at this stage. Based on my promise to get back to him within two weeks, he agreed to hold off suing.

While gathering the facts, it struck me that my client might have a great legal defense. I asked Sarah, a first-year associate attorney with whom I had not yet worked, to do the research. Sarah said, "I have a few assignments to complete. Will Thursday suffice?"

"Sure," I said, thinking to myself, "I can then call opposing counsel on Friday, which is the last day within the two weeks."

Preoccupied with other work, I didn't notice that Thursday came and went without word from Sarah. On Friday morning, another client had an employee relations problem detonate at the workplace. While responding to the frantic emails and phone calls, I completely forgot about getting back to opposing counsel on the other matter. And I heard nothing from Sarah.

The weekend passed, and Monday morning I left on a business trip. After I checked into my hotel Monday evening, the thought struck me like a blow: "Oh #@$!%&! I forgot to call opposing counsel on Friday. I'd better call him first thing tomorrow morning so that he doesn't file the complaint. I'd hate to have my client sued because I dropped the ball!"

This thought immediately led to another: "Oh #@$!%&! I never heard from Sarah! I don't want to have that conversation with counsel until I know whether or not we have this defense. #@$!%&!"

I immediately emailed Sarah. "What's the answer?" I demanded. "I'm past the date I promised to respond to plaintiff's counsel. I'm afraid he'll go ahead and file the complaint against our client—a very bad and embarrassing thing for our firm."

Sarah responded shortly thereafter with an apology and promise she'd have an answer by morning.

After a fitful night's sleep, I awoke Tuesday morning and sure enough, Sarah had emailed me her answer along with a research memorandum. According to Sarah, we had a great defense. Eureka! However, as I read her memorandum, I detected a potentially serious error in Sarah's analysis. I thought, "If I call the attorney, assert the defense and am wrong, my credibility will be shot. But if I wait to call until I've figured out the answer, he may sue my client in the meantime."

I decided to call the attorney, but instead of responding to his client's claim, I apologized for the delay and promised I'd respond by Friday. Somewhat grudgingly, he said okay.

I then emailed Sarah my concerns about her conclusion and asked her to reexamine. Later that day, she emailed me. "I'm very sorry. I made a mistake. Under the facts of this case, our client does *not* have this defense."

At that moment, steam started coming out of my ears. I thought, "First she misses the deadline. Then she gives me the wrong answer!" After cooling down a bit, I asked myself a question that has often stopped me from doing something really stupid, "As a coach, what would I advise me to do?"

Taking my advice, after I returned from my trip, I visited Sarah in her office. She was visibly nervous. I said, "Before discussing what happened, I'd like to share a couple of things with you.

"Over the years, two characteristics have distinguished associates I've valued highly from those with whom I've struggled. The first is timeliness. When associates own responsibility for deadlines, it enables me to do my job better. When they don't, either the responsibility stays on my back, which slows me down and burdens me, or worse—we risk disaster.

"The second characteristic is that when associates think they've found the answer, they ask themselves, 'What might I have missed?' or 'How might I be wrong?' Every lawyer I know, myself included, has made the mistake of prematurely disabling his or her inner critic when they think they have the answer. They don't take the next step of challenging their legal or factual assumptions as if they were their own opposing counsel."

I said, "What are your thoughts, Sarah?"

She paused and said, "I clearly blew it on both points. I got really busy late last week and forgot the assignment. When I got your email on Monday evening, I panicked and immediately started researching. I worked late into the night.

"I was so happy when I thought I found the answer you were hoping for, I said to myself, 'Given the good news, maybe he'll forgive my lateness.' There was no questioning inner voice at that point."

Sarah added, "In fact, I think the two characteristics are connected. Missing the first one set me up to miss the second. Working late and in kind of panic mode made me more susceptible to mistakes."

"I agree," I said. "I see the connection too. However, the point is not to dwell on the past. It's to change how we work in the future. Frankly, since you and I hadn't worked together before, there's no reason I couldn't or shouldn't have shared these points at the outset. In fact, I don't want you to hesitate to tell me if there's something I can do that will improve your effectiveness. After all, if you're successful, I'm successful, and the client's successful."

Thereafter, Sarah and I continued to work well together and are friends to this day.

MORAL OF THE STORY

I can think of at least five morals to this story.

When employees fall short of expectations, we have a tendency to assign blame. We jump into corrective action mode. Yet a more nuanced and holistic approach involves becoming curious as opposed to judgmental. There's a fundamental difference between asking, "What happened?" and "How come you screwed up?" Until an employee has demonstrated through repeated or egregious missteps that you have an individual problem, a better approach is to ask what collectively might be done differently going forward that would enable your expectations to be met.

Similar to my observations about Samuel in "Performance Review Follies," it's better to discuss performance expectations upfront as opposed to waiting until after the fact. After my experience with Sarah, I started to make it a practice whenever I worked with someone for the first time to share the key behavioral characteristics I value before they began their work. Results have validated this practice.

This story reminds us of the importance of the What/ Why Ratio ("Managing Millennials Is the Pits!"). When I gave Sarah the assignment, I told her what I wanted but neglected to mention why. Had I taken an additional minute to share with her the game plan—why her answer on Thursday would be needed because Friday was the deadline to respond to opposing counsel—she'd have been less likely to forget. Among other benefits, knowing the "why" behind the "what" helps sync the task with one's memory.

My assignment to Sarah is a good illustration of how one could use Same Day Summaries ("Texas Wes"). Taking only a few minutes, I could have sent Sarah a quick email following our conversation that covered the points of what she was going to do by when, and why. Better yet, to give her a greater sense of ownership, I could've asked Sarah to do the summary. Had either of us done one, I can virtually guarantee the problem wouldn't have arisen in the first place.

When faced with a frustrating employee situation, a great way to settle yourself down and take a constructive approach to dealing with it is to ask yourself a question like I asked myself before confronting Sarah. Behavioral psychologists have coined a term, the Solomon Paradox, based on the story of Solomon, who was known as the wisest of kings when advising others yet whose own personal decisions proved utterly disastrous. When we're on the hot seat, we tend to behave differently than how we'd advise someone we care deeply about in the same circumstances. We gather less information, identify fewer options, and are more rigid in our thinking. When personally dealing with a challenging situation, you don't have to be an executive coach like me to ask yourself, "How would I advise someone I care about if they faced this situation?" Just as I did with Sarah, you'll probably handle it a lot more effectively.

CHAPTER
4

DISCIPLINE & DISCHARGE

THE ICE BENEATH THE WAVES: AN EXPENSIVE LESSON IN PROCRASTINATION
(The Cost of Avoidance)

My client employed a salesman, Edward. His performance over 12 years could best be described as, "Once in a great while comes somewhat close to meeting expectations."

Various corrective measures had been attempted over the years: retraining, coaching, counseling, performance improvement plans, even changing supervisors. Yet other than occasional fleeting improvement, the problems remained.

Finally, after years of low sales, alienated coworkers, and numerous customer complaints, the company decided to fire Edward. However, because it had tolerated him for so long and didn't get its ducks in row before acting, and because he was now well into his 50s, the company ended up having to defend an age discrimination claim.

After months of litigation, the company agreed to pay a settlement to avoid incurring further litigation cost and risk of adverse judgment. Total claim expense was just over $100,000.

I subsequently learned that Edward's replacement, working the same territory and in her first year, outsold Edward's best year by nearly $200,000. In subsequent years, the performance gap grew even larger. In addition, customer complaints and defections virtually ceased, and co-workers described her as a good team player.

Now get this: After we settled Edward's claim, the company's CEO complained to me about the high cost of litigation and having had to spend $100,000 to get rid of a lousy employee. "The legal system is a pain in the butt," he said.

However, the CEO never did the math regarding what it cost his company to continue employing Edward: how much revenue it had lost, how many customers had defected to competitors, and how many employees Edward had alienated. In other words, the CEO never calculated how many multiples of the litigation cost had already been lost by keeping Edward employed for 12 years.

MORAL OF THE STORY

This case is not that unusual. Employers tolerate problematic employees for years, never assessing the cost of keeping them employed. When they finally act and the employee sues, they howl about legal fees and paying for settlements. Yet by focusing on the iceberg's tip—the visible one-tenth—they miss the rest of it, the nine-tenths of their true loss in allowing the status quo to remain for so long.

The lesson of this story is that if you have an employee problem, put together a game plan now. Don't wait for the "I can't take it anymore!" moment.

It's your call. Do you want to delay action so that you can eventually kvetch about the tip of the iceberg? Or do you want to do something now about the growing body of ice beneath your waves?

TOUGH TRIAL LAWYER TURNS TIMID
(Beware the Instinct to Avoid)

When I started my first law job, Alfred was my mentor. Our firm's chief trial lawyer and a former college athlete, Alfred stood well over six feet tall, had broad shoulders, a thick beard, and a deep, booming voice. With over 100 jury trials under his belt, Alfred thrived on conflict and high drama.

Alfred and I had adjacent offices and shared a legal secretary, Susan. Although Susan was pleasant, her typing was slow and error prone. Also, she had a tendency to misfile documents and mistranscribe telephone messages.

Alfred and I discussed our mutual frustration. "Should we sit down with Susan and let her know?" I asked.

"No," Alfred replied. "We'll tell Liz and she'll talk to Susan." (Liz was our firm's administrator.) "That's Liz's job," Alfred added.

After we went upstairs to Liz's office and shared our frustrations, Liz met with Susan. As a result, there was discernible behavior change: Susan no longer smiled or greeted us. But the performance problems remained.

One day, Alfred said to me, "Enough's enough. Susan's got to go."

"How should we handle it?" I asked.

"Easy. We'll tell Liz and she'll handle it."

The axe hadn't yet fallen when I returned from lunch a few days later. I got off the elevator and headed down the hall to my office. I saw Alfred coming out of his office and heading my way, almost at a trot. He was moving fast.

As our paths crossed, I said, "What's up?"

He looked at me, and in an urgent whisper said, "Liz is coming downstairs to do the deed. I'm getting the hell out of here!"

With that, Alfred bolted past me toward the elevator bank.

I took another step toward my office and stopped. After a moment's hesitation, I wheeled around and yelled to Alfred, "Hold that elevator!"

MORAL OF THE STORY

There's a good analogy between downhill skiing and managing employees.

In skiing, beginners must overcome a natural, intuitive, and seemingly self-protective instinct. When at the top of the slope facing downhill, beginners are naturally fearful of going too fast, out of control, and crashing. As a result, they resist the gravitational pull of the downhill slope by leaning back on their skis. Invariably, however, giving in to this instinct produces the very thing they fear. They go too fast, out of control, and crash.

So what do ski instructors teach? The opposite. Put your weight forward on your skis, toward that downhill slope. This makes no sense at first and seems a sure recipe for disaster, yet if you stay with it, you'll discover it works. Only by doing the opposite of what your instinct tells you to do can you control speed and direction and stay upright.

There's also a natural, intuitive, and seemingly self-protective instinct in management, one that's equally misguided. It's to avoid problematic workplace situations. We can't predict the outcome if we confront the problem directly, so we lean back on our skis in hopes the problem will go away on its own or someone else will fix it. Yet almost inevitably the opposite happens. Avoidance makes the problem worse and increases the likelihood that what we fear will come to pass: a bad ending to a workplace relationship.

Fortunately, managers can use that avoidance instinct the same way skiers use the lean-back-on-their-skis instinct—as a trigger to do the opposite. That gnarly employee problem you have, the one you've been putting off dealing with? Instead of moving it off the agenda or to the bottom of the agenda, move it to the top of your agenda. Develop a game plan and execute it. Now.

For a long time, Alfred and I had repressed our frustrations with Susan's performance. We said nothing to her. And then when things hit the breaking point, we still didn't talk to her. It was easier in the moment to have Liz do it. And you can see how successful that approach was.

Had Alfred and I put our weight forward on our skis, we'd have been prompt, candid, direct, and specific with Susan about our expectations, the gap in meeting them, and what was needed to close the gap. Had we done so, I predict one of two things would have occurred: (1) Susan would have closed the performance gap to our satisfaction or (2) a transition to a new secretary would have happened a lot sooner, and without bitterness or rancor.

And neither of us would have had to run for the elevator.

DISCHARGE FROM FOUR DOORS DOWN
(Email Is Not the Way to Convey an Emotionally Sensitive Message)

The company had grown to where it needed to hire a CFO. Following a nationwide search, it hired Ralph, a Harvard MBA. Terms were negotiated, a contract signed, and Ralph moved his family across the country for his new job.

Shortly after his arrival, Ralph participated in his first executive committee meeting. During the meeting, he made a comment that bothered the CEO, Jordan. Jordan said nothing at the time. However, after he got back to his office, he used the then fairly new communication tool called email. Here's what he wrote:

> **To:** Ralph
> **From:** Jordan
> **Subject:** Today's Executive Committee Meeting
> **Sent:** October 14, 1997, 10:14 AM
>
> I was disappointed with some of your comments in today's meeting about our expansion plan. I'm not sure you fully understand what we're trying to accomplish.
>
> *Click Send.*

Ralph responded with a message of his own.

> **To:** Jordan
> **From:** Ralph
> **Subject:** Today's Executive Committee Meeting
> **Sent:** October 14, 1997, 10:39 AM
>
> You are mistaken Jordan. I fully understand the Company's business objectives. However, I was hired to ensure that they are pursued within a framework of sound and proper business practices, and with a view to protecting the company's assets and preserving shareholder value. I'm simply doing my job.
>
> *Click Send.*

Jordan stewed on this message for a while, then composed the following:

> **To:** Ralph
> **From:** Jordan
> **Subject:** Today's Executive Committee Meeting
> **Sent:** October 14, 1997, 11:49 AM
>
> THE HELL I'M MISTAKEN! I just need team players who support what I'm trying to accomplish as opposed to getting in my way!

Click Send.

Given the heat in Jordan's message, Ralph decided it would be better not to reply.

Things quieted down for a while. The two men never talked about their email exchange but went on, at least to all appearances, to business as usual. However, it didn't take long before another disagreement touched off a new round of emails. Jordan ended that exchange with the following:

> **To:** Ralph
> **From:** Jordan
> **Cc:** Human Resources
> **Subject:** Moving on!
> **Sent:** October 28, 1997, 2:43 PM
>
> It has become increasingly clear to me that as a company, we cannot succeed with you as its CFO. We made a

mistake when we hired you, which I'm rectifying today. Our HR Director will process your termination. Best of luck in the future.

Click Send.

After Ralph received this message, he didn't click Reply. Instead, he clicked Forward. (You can guess to whom.)

Acrimonious negotiations ensued between the parties and their attorneys regarding Ralph's threatened breach-of-contract and whistleblower claims. Eventually, a deal was cut. It wasn't cheap.

Regarding Jordan's use of email to convey his issues with Ralph, it wasn't due to geographic separation where the executives worked in different cities. During their entire series of increasingly negative exchanges, Jordan and Ralph were only four office doors apart.

MORAL OF THE STORY

This story highlights another aspect of the avoidance instinct discussed in the preceding story. Few of us enjoy face-to-face conversations on difficult subjects. Thus, email seems a convenient, less-stressful way to convey tough messages.

Yet it's a big mistake to inform an employee of problematic behavior without speaking to and looking at the person at the same time. First, your lack of directness will likely be perceived as disrespect. Second, your attempt at conveying a sensitive message via writing is likely to be construed in ways you don't foresee. Third, you won't have a real-time opportunity to head off misunderstanding or negative emotions; instead, the employee will read, reread, and re-reread your words, letting them fester and stew.

I coach managers on how to avoid dissing employees by "DISing" them. That means being direct, immediate, and specific. Email doesn't satisfy the direct test. Nor does a text, letter, memo, or voicemail message. Rather, it requires a face-to-face exchange. The avoidance instinct says that's the least comfortable option yet to achieve positive results, it's by far the most effective.

Instead of waiting until he was back in his office, Jordan should have pulled Ralph aside after the meeting and shared his concerns directly. He would have had a far greater chance to achieve a positive outcome had he done so. But the temptation to take the easy way out—put fingers on keyboard while alone in the office—proved too much.

As I explained in "Texas Wes and the Same Day Summary," email does have an important role in workplace communication. That's when it serves as an after-the-fact follow-up summary of key points discussed in a face-to-face conversation and not as a substitute for it.

THE UNION MAN AND THE WHITE LIE
(Straying from the Truth Is Never a Good Idea)

Mick was a stocky, grizzled, 58-year-old dockworker at a trucking company. He combined low productivity with a chip-on-the-shoulder attitude. Over the years, he'd been repeatedly passed over for advancement but allowed to keep his job. Mick was passionately pro-union and frustrated by the fact that unionization efforts at his trucking terminal had been unsuccessful, in contrast to the company's terminals in other states.

Mick punctuated his mediocre work performance with two incidents of misconduct. The first occurred at an all-employees meeting at which the operations manager announced a new policy regarding restrictions on PTO (paid time off). Mick unloaded on the operations manager: "If we had a union here, we wouldn't have to put up with this bullshit policy, put out by bullshit managers at a bullshit company!"

Company management wanted to fire Mick for this outburst. However, worries about potential union and other legal trouble led it to issue Mick a disciplinary write-up instead.

Several months later, after the union called a strike at a company terminal in another state, Mick attempted to organize a sympathy picket at his terminal. Among the employees he lobbied was a young dockworker, Bill. Mick asked him, "If a picket line gets set up, will you support it?"

Bill replied, "Sorry, Mick, I've got a mortgage and car payments to make, and my wife is pregnant. I can't afford to lose my job. I'd have to cross the picket line."

Mick asked, "That house of yours, do you have insurance on it?"

"Yes, of course."

"What about your car?"

After a pause and a quizzical look, Bill said, "Uh, yes."

Mick then asked, "That wife of yours, do you have insurance on her?"

Bill didn't answer. Instead, he walked away.

Bill did not report this incident to management. He was too frightened. However, an employee overheard Bill telling a friend at work about it and asking him in earnest, "Do you think Mick's serious?" The employee reported what he heard to management, which conducted an investigation.

When confronted, Mick admitted asking Bill those questions, but said, "I didn't mean anything by it. I was only joking with the kid."

Management wanted to fire Mick, but fears of union or other legal trouble again induced it to settle for a disciplinary write-up.

There were no further incidents with Mick. His work effort remained mediocre, but he confined his inflammatory comments to low-volume muttering.

A subsequent business downturn resulted in a company-wide directive to cut operation costs by 20 percent. This included a reduction in force (RIF) at Mick's terminal.

Management evaluated employees from best to worst, letting go the ones at the bottom.

By all accounts except perhaps his own, Mick was easily the worst employee. Repressing its glee, management informed Mick that he was being let go as part of the RIF.

Mick responded by filing a claim of age discrimination with the state antidiscrimination agency. He cited the fact that he was the oldest dockworker, had more seniority than most, yet was the first chosen to be fired.

The agency scheduled a fact-finding conference for the parties to present their positions and evidence. As the company's attorney, I felt confident we could show that Mick's age had nothing to do with his termination; rather, it was his demonstrably low productivity and misbehavior.

At the conference, however, my client and I were in for a surprise. Mick walked in with a boom box music machine. He plugged it into a wall socket and popped in a cassette tape.

(Note to millennials: This case happened a long time ago.)

We heard three recordings of conversations Mick had with management: one with his immediate supervisor, one with the operations manager, and one with the terminal general manager. None of them knew they were being recorded. Here's what we heard:

Mick to his immediate supervisor: "Hey boss: Is the work I'm doing okay with you?" Supervisor to Mick: "Yeah sure. I've got no issues with you."

Mick to the operations manager: "Remember that meeting where I got a little hot under the collar and said some things

I probably shouldn't have? Well, I didn't really mean the stuff I said. I'm fine with you. Are we cool?" Operations manager to Mick: "Don't worry about it. It's over and done with as far as I'm concerned."

Mick to the general manager: "You understand I was only joking with Bill, don't you? I mean, I know I shouldn't have. Kids these days, you never know how they're gonna take stuff." General manager to Mick: "Sure. I understand. Things are fine now. It's in the past."

After Mick hit the machine's stop button, I called a time out to confer with my witnesses. Despite what they'd said on the tape, all three managers insisted that Mick's low productivity, profane explosion at the operations manager's meeting, and threat to Bill were critical factors in the decision to select him for the RIF.

So what reasons did they give for lying to Mick? They said it was the easiest thing to do at the time. It got Mick to stop pestering them.

For Mick, management's white lies turned green. We'd gone to the hearing adamant that Mick wasn't going to get a nickel. However, these taped conversations altered our assessment. We ended up agreeing to a fairly generous severance package in exchange for Mick's permanently leaving the company and releasing all claims.

MORAL OF THE STORY

Benjamin Franklin said it best: "Honesty is the best policy." This is particularly true when honesty seems least convenient. The managers at this company valued honesty and integrity. Yet they told lies. They rationalized that circumstances warranted an exception to "Honesty is the best policy."

As in the two preceding stories, the culprit is once again that seductive, seemingly self-protective instinct to avoid. Lies may work in the short term. Our Micks may get out of our faces and temporarily stop pestering us. In my experience, however, the long-term costs and risks of avoidance far outweigh the short-term benefits.

In my law practice years, I think I heard just about every workplace lie you could imagine: lies by commission (outright falsehoods), lies by omission (technically true statements that mislead by omitting key facts), spoken lies, and written lies (the performance review is a common example of the latter). Almost invariably, the explanations (rationalizations) relate to avoidance.

Here's my favorite: In an employment-discrimination lawsuit, one of the employer's managers admitted to me that he had lied to the employee who was now suing the company. I asked him, "Why did you lie?"

The manager said, "Because I was afraid if I told the truth, we might end up getting sued."

And look where we ended up.

A BLACK AND WHITE LESSON IN CONSISTENCY
(Get Your Ducks in a Row Before You Act)

In cubicles pressed against each other like sardines, a large group of telemarketers worked the phones. The noise could be deafening.

In adjacent cubicles sat two young men, large men, with thick necks. One was black, the other white. Their voices were loud, so loud they interfered with each other's calls. What was their solution? Raise their voices, of course.

Frustration built until one said to the other, "Lower your %$&!# voice! I can't hear a $%#&! thing!"

To which the other man responded, "$%#&! What are you talking about? You have the loudest %$&#! voice in the whole room! Why don't you lower your $%#&! voice?"

Soon the two men were on their feet, yelling, gesturing, practically foaming at the mouth. Expletives filled the air.

Activity in the room stopped. All eyes were on them.

Finally, one man raised his hands, gestured to the other, and said in a low, hard voice, "Enough of this. Let's you and I take it *outside*."

A coworker stepped between them. Others intervened as well. No punches were thrown.

Following an investigation, management decided to reprimand one of the men and fire the other. The reprimanded employee was white, the terminated employee black.

Following his termination, the ex-employee hired a

prominent plaintiff's attorney and filed a race discrimination claim with the Equal Employment Opportunity Commission (EEOC). The commission scheduled a mediation session to give the parties an early settlement opportunity. It did not start well, however.

"This is an outrageous case of blatant race discrimination!" the employee's attorney thundered. "Your company should be ashamed of itself!"

The attorney presented his client's settlement demand: full reinstatement with all lost salary and benefits repaid, plus payment of attorney's fees and $50,000 "to compensate for my client's emotional distress. Otherwise, we will be happy to file a lawsuit in federal court where we are confident of being awarded a far greater sum of money."

Now it was my turn. "I think I understand your position," I began. "You believe there's race discrimination because the black employee got fired while the white employee kept his job, and the decision-makers were white. In your view, this inconsistency in treatment can only be explained by racial prejudice.

"However, there's some information I'd like to share with you that I believe will show something quite different—that what appears inconsistent is actually the opposite."

I gave the attorney a copy of a company policy that stated, "Acts or threats of violence will subject the offender to termination on a first offense." I also gave him a copy of the acknowledgment page his client had signed, which stated, "I have reviewed and agree to follow the policies in this handbook." I then said:

"This explains the difference in disciplinary action. Before a decision was made, the company conducted an investigation. It interviewed the two employees in question as well as eyewitnesses. Based on its investigation, management concluded that both employees were at fault for their disruptive behavior. However, only one person threatened violence. That was your client.

"Also, you should know that there was a prior incident where an employee threatened another with violence and was fired on a first offense. That employee was white.

"So," I concluded, "for the company to have behaved other than it did would have been inconsistent with both policy and practice."

The energy on the other side of the table seemed to fade. The attorney requested additional documentation, which I agreed to provide, and the mediation session concluded without an offer of reinstatement or money.

I didn't hear from the attorney until two weeks before the deadline would run out for filing a lawsuit. "Look," he said, "my client is willing to waive reinstatement. We asked for $50,000 before but we'll accept $5,000."

"I'm sorry," I said. "The company has made it clear that I'm not authorized to offer any sum of money to settle a claim. It has a practice of not settling claims where it doesn't think it did wrong."

Two weeks went by. No filing. Claim over.

MORAL OF THE STORY

In employment-discrimination litigation, often the fight is about consistency versus inconsistency. Plaintiffs use management inconsistency to argue that its stated reasons for its actions are false—a pretext for concealed, unlawful motives.

The inconsistency trap is easy to fall into. All too often, management has avoided dealing with an employee problem for a long time but has now reached the breaking point. Immediate action must be taken. In its haste, management overlooks problematic facts such as positive performance reviews or policy provisions its action will contradict.

Before it acted, management in this case wisely asked the three "ducks in a row" questions:

- ▸ Have similar situations arisen?
- ▸ What do the documents say?
- ▸ Can we show there is no inconsistency?

Answers to these questions pointed clearly to what action needed to be taken. Although there was an apparent inconsistency in treatment of the two employees, closer scrutiny revealed the opposite. Because the company could show how and why its actions were consistent, it escaped an expensive experience in the U.S. judicial system.

BONUS MORAL OF THE STORY

As well as the employer handled the situation, there's one thing it might have done differently, which probably would have prevented the original claim from having been made. When it let the African American employee go, it said nothing about the disciplinary action it was taking with the white employee. As you can predict, the black employee soon learned that his white coworker had kept his job. This fueled a sense of outrage, which prompted him to seek a plaintiff's attorney.

Although the company made the right disciplinary decision, I would have recommended explaining the reasons for the difference in treatment at the time of termination. Otherwise, you leave the fired employee to speculate, which, as I explained in "The New Cadillac, the Fur Coat, and the Confidentiality Clause," is almost always worse than reality.

Instead of firing the employee in summary fashion, I would have shared with him copies of the antiviolence policy and his acknowledgment page. I would have explained the investigative finding based on eyewitness statements and the company practice to terminate on first offense. Without identifying anyone, I would have mentioned the prior incident, including the race of the person who was previously fired. Based on my experience, I'm confident no claim would have been filed. The fired employee would have moved on quietly to find other employment.

But then you'd have missed out on this story.

A TALE OF TWO LAYOFFS

TALE #1: "I Can't Log In"
(How You Fire Can Be More Important Than Whom You Fire)

For 26 years, George worked for the same company. One morning, after parking his car in the employee lot and taking the elevator to his fourth-floor office, George booted up his computer. He attempted to log in, but the user name/password combination didn't work. He tried twice more without success. As he reached for the telephone to call IT, he noticed his message light was on. The message was from Betty in human resources: "George, please call me as soon as you get in. It's important."

He called Betty. She answered and said, "I'll be right there."

Betty arrived at George's office with a broad-shouldered man in a dark suit George had never seen before. Betty introduced them. "This is Bill from security," she said. "George, I have some bad news. Due to a business downturn, we've had to eliminate several positions, including yours. I'm sorry, but today is your last day."

Betty handed him his final paycheck along with a letter explaining the impact of his termination on his health insurance, retirement, and other benefits. She also handed him a contract and said, "This document is a separation agreement and release of claims. If you decide to sign it, the company will pay you four weeks of severance. You can take it home and decide later."

Betty explained the reason for Bill's presence: "He's here to help you gather your personal things and see you to your car. Again, I'm sorry, George. I wish you the very best of success in the future." With that, she walked out of his office.

George was too shocked to say anything. After a few minutes of silence, George began looking around his office for personal items. In boxes Bill handed him, George began packing: family photographs, personal books, company mementos, a couple of plants, and his Chicago Cubs coffee mug.

With Bill looking on to make sure no company property was included, George soon had his things boxed up and ready to go. Bill carried one box while George carried the other. After walking down a hallway, they had to cross an open area where other employees were present. George saw several colleagues, but they didn't make eye contact. Nobody said anything. There were tears in George's eyes.

After helping George put the boxes in his car, Bill said, "Nice to meet you. Goodbye."

"Goodbye," replied George, as he started his car. On the drive home, he thought, "Why did I say 'Goodbye?' I should have said, 'Go to hell!'"

Neither George nor his wife were impressed with the company's four weeks' severance offer. He told her, "That's all they offer me after 26 years of service? I'm 54 years old, we still have a kid in college and a mortgage!" George didn't say aloud the fact that his wife had health problems, although this was very much on their minds.

Shock and dismay turned to anger, "They wouldn't even let me say goodbye. Instead they walked me out of there in front of coworkers like some kind of criminal! And they let me know I've been fired by locking me out of my computer!"

George's cousin, a tax attorney, referred him to a lawyer who specialized in representing employees. After the attorney's attempts to negotiate a better severance package for George were unavailing, George filed a lawsuit in federal court alleging age discrimination.

After two years of litigation, the case went to trial. The jury was sympathetic to George and offended by the manner in which management let him go. Also, George's attorney was able to introduce evidence of inconsistencies, with younger employees in his department keeping their jobs despite fewer years of service and less-favorable performance evaluations.

The jury awarded George $1.6 million in damages. The company appealed. After another year of wrangling in the legal system, the parties reached a settlement. The company ended up paying $850,000 to settle George's claims. By then, it had spent nearly $300,000 in litigation costs and attorneys' fees.

TALE #2: Too Much Information Is Better Than Not Enough (Sharing Bad News Can Produce Good Results)

We sat around my client's conference room table: five members of the company's executive team and me. I'd been asked to do a risk assessment of a RIF they intended to conduct.

The company had purchased a large tract of land near St. Louis and had begun construction of a distribution center. Once the St. Louis facility was operational, the company intended to close its existing facility outside of Atlanta. Only a few Atlanta employees would be offered relocation packages. The rest, 460 employees, would be let go.

In addition to legal compliance issues, topics of discussion included what the company should say to the Atlanta employees about the impending change.

"Nothing," said one executive. "Not until we tell them that their employment has been terminated."

Another executive said, "We need them to perform right up until St. Louis goes operational. Otherwise, we're going to have big customer headaches."

They turned to me, "Jathan, what do you advise?"

"Well," I said. "I've had experiences where employees were told well in advance of their termination date and didn't behave badly. I've also had experiences where the company's attempt to keep things secret backfired. Leaked information combined with negative rumors and speculation created a toxic work environment.

"I think if you're upfront with the Atlanta employees about what you're doing and why, and how they fit into the plan, it will work better than playing your cards close to the chest. With the severance you're willing to pay based on their continuing to work up to a release date you set, I think you'll get the performance you need."

An energetic discussion ensued. Eventually the executive team agreed to follow the approach I outlined, although after the meeting, one executive pulled me aside and said, "This damn well better work!"

We put together a game plan that included management holding a series of meetings to explain to employees what the company was doing, why, and how it would impact them. The company conveyed additional information through its intranet and via periodic emails from the CEO. Employees were encouraged to ask questions. If management didn't yet have answers, it promised to respond as soon as it could.

Not surprisingly, many Atlanta employees were unhappy about the change. "Why St. Louis?" "What's wrong with keeping things the way they are?" Some employees were upset that a few were offered relocation packages while most were not, prompting some "Why not me?" questions.

Management didn't duck any questions and patiently explained its reasons. When disagreement continued, it acknowledged a legitimate difference of opinion. "We're trying to use our best business judgment to keep our company competitive. You may not agree, and there may be better ways to do things. But these are decisions we felt we had to make, and we wanted to share them with you in advance so that you at least understood what we were doing and why, and had time to plan."

Ultimately, 460 employees lost their jobs. That's 460 potential lawsuits to defend. However, it didn't work out that way. Not even close. Following the plant closure, there were no lawsuits. There wasn't even a single attorney demand letter.

Instead, employees reliably performed their jobs until their release dates. They signed the separation agreements, accepted the severance pay, and moved on. Productivity did not suffer.

A facility manager shared a story that sums things up:

"I got a call from a customer. He said, 'I want to tell you how impressed I was by one of your employees. We had a problem with a shipment, and he jumped on it, fixed the problem, made sure we were satisfied, and remained cooperative and friendly throughout.

"'I complimented him on his excellent service and attitude. He said he appreciated the compliment, especially since he would be out of a job in a month and could use the encouragement. I was shocked, and then amazed we received such great service from somebody who knew he was about to lose his job!'"

MORAL OF THE STORY

These two stories illustrate the difference in philosophy and approach employers commonly take in handling layoffs and RIFs. Unfortunately, the first story is more typical. The employer takes an almost adversarial approach, showing little or no trust in employees, sharing as little information as possible and as late as possible, and acting essentially without regard for the impact on employees, including their dignity.

By contrast, and as shown in the second story, being upfront in sharing sensitive, difficult information tends to send a message of trust and respect. It upholds employee dignity, which often distinguishes workplace layoffs that go well from those that don't. In my career, I've dealt with numerous layoffs, RIFs, and other downsizings. In reflecting on the ones that went smoothly, it strikes me that it was not so much a question of who got laid off or what the business justifications were. Rather, it was the manner in which departing employees were treated.

If you've ever been unfortunate enough to be caught up in a job reduction, you probably understand. When faced with the hardship, dislocation, and anxiety of losing your job, the last thing you need is to have the blow accompanied by negation of your dignity or self-worth.

Edgar Allan Poe captured this sentiment 170 years ago with the opening to his story "The Cask of Amontillado": "The thousand injuries of Fortunado I had borne as I best could. But when he ventured upon insult, I vowed revenge."

Taking away someone's job is inflicting an injury; don't add insult.

CONVERTING HUMAN RESOURCES FROM COP TO COACH (How to Combine the Business Case with Employee Risk Analysis)

Following a workshop I conducted, the company's human resources director, Mary, invited me to sit in on a meeting she had scheduled with a senior executive, Morton. He wanted to fire a long-time employee in his department, Jerry, and sought Mary's backing.

For years, Jerry had underperformed, alienating co-workers, disappointing and even offending customers. Morton explained that he'd given Jerry extra coaching and counseling, had tried performance improvement plans, and had even switched Jerry to different supervisors. However, no sustained positive change had occurred.

The executive explained that there was a new and real urgency: Technological and market changes had created industry upheaval. Morton cited his boss, the company's CEO, who had recently said, "We can no longer afford to tolerate dead wood."

Morton said, "It doesn't get much deader than Jerry."

Moreover, Morton explained, a competitor had been raiding employees in his department and had succeeded in recruiting away two of his best. "Nobody wants to work with Jerry, which makes us vulnerable to our competitor's raids," Morton said. "We simply can't afford to carry this guy any longer. We've got to get him out of here!"

Mary spoke for the first time. "What is your documentation?" she asked.

Not surprisingly, the documents weren't very helpful.

"But what about the performance improvement plans?" Morton asked defensively.

"They're not current," Mary replied. "Besides, technically speaking, they were complied with."

"Yeah, but in his last performance review, his supervisor checked 'needs improvement' in several places," Morton said.

"Checking 'needs improvement' on a performance review is not the same as a performance improvement plan, and it doesn't constitute clear disciplinary notice that an employee faces termination of employment."

"I recently told Jerry that he needed to look for another job."

"You may have told him that, but that's not the same as supportive documentation."

Things were getting tense when Mary turned to me and said, "Jathan, do you have anything to say?"

"I like to start by making sure I understand the business case," I said. I turned to Morton and attempted to summarize the problem from his perspective: the long, frustrating years of employing Jerry, the failed attempts at improvement, the heightened sense of urgency due to industry upheaval, and the fresh crisis caused by a competitor's talent raids.

After Morton confirmed that I'd accurately summarized the situation, I said:

"Now, let's examine your desired action through a risk analysis checklist. There are four prongs:

- Would the termination be substantively fair?
- Would it be procedurally fair?
- Would it be consistent?
- Are there any complicating factors?

"As for the first prong, I'd say you've made a strong case that it would be substantively fair to let Jerry go. It's not a personality conflict or a manager's vendetta. You've given him repeated opportunities to improve, but he remains unwilling or unable to close the gap.

"The next item is procedural fairness. Has adequate notice been given so that firing Jerry won't be a surprise? From my experience, I can say that employees will surprise you with how surprised they are when the hammer finally comes down. From the manager's perspective, they should have seen it coming from miles away. But not from the employee's perspective.

"Also, you'll be surprised at how your good employees, the ones you want to keep, will identify with an underperforming employee if they feel he wasn't given fair notice before being fired. They'll think, 'Maybe that'll happen to me some day,' which is not helpful for employee engagement or talent retention.

"To avoid such surprise, clear advance oral and written notice should be given. Unfortunately, Morton, I see real problems with this prong of the checklist. But let's continue.

"The next question is whether firing Jerry would be consistent with company policy, procedure, and practice. Consistency isn't just about protecting the company against workplace claims. It's about supporting a culture where employees feel they will be treated fairly. When management bypasses its own policies or procedures because a particular situation strikes it as compelling, it often pays a price in creating the sense that leadership can't be trusted. Obviously, that's also not a good thing for employee engagement or talent retention.

"I've got concerns on the consistency prong as well. Firing Jerry now would appear inconsistent with the disciplinary procedure stated in the handbook as well as past disciplinary practice."

"Finally," I said, "in terms of potential complicating factors, there's the legal risk. In this case, Jerry is well over 40, and I understand he could be replaced by someone well under that age. That fact, plus the problems with checklist items (2) and (3) could easily result in a painfully expensive litigation experience."

The room was silent.

I said, "Clients often find it helpful to analyze legal risk in relation to business costs and benefits. I use an equation, $V=LM$, where the Value of a contemplated action is determined by assessing the Likelihood of its occurring multiplied by its Magnitude. For example, think of comparing a 50 percent risk of losing $10 ($5 in present value) versus a 30 percent risk of losing $100 ($30 in present value).

"This approach leads to creating multiple options and weighing them against each other. I like to start by identifying options on each end of the risk spectrum and then looking at something in between.

"In this case, the high-risk option would be to fire Jerry now. That would cut off the business cost of continuing to employ him. However, it would maximize legal risk—the Likelihood that Jerry would sue and collect a high Magnitude of money.

"The low-risk option would be to continue tolerating Jerry as best you can. That essentially eliminates the legal risk (LxM=0), but for the reasons you described, it would come at a high business cost, including the risk of further talent loss or your CEO becoming very unhappy with you.

"A risk option in between might involve bringing Jerry to the edge of discharge while leaving yourself some wiggle room. For example, you could lay out in detail why it's in his best interest to leave the company. And perhaps incentivize him with a severance/release offer. That approach has some legal risk but also creates a decent chance of getting Jerry out of the company sooner versus later, and without legal or other trouble."

At that point, Morton and Mary agreed to meet the following morning and develop a game plan.

A few months later, Mary called me. She said:

"We agreed on a middle option. Together, we created one of the most comprehensive performance improvement plans I've ever seen. We met with Jerry and walked him through his entire employment history, pointing out the many failures and failed attempts to make things work. We told him we were at a crossroads; the company could no longer tolerate the status quo. It therefore seemed to us that the best thing would be for Jerry to find other employment. If he agreed, we'd be willing to provide some severance benefits to help with his transition. Otherwise, if he wanted a last-chance opportunity, we'd need to see his proposed corrective action plan.

"We also said it was an either/or proposition—either he could elect severance or he could attempt a last-chance correction plan. If he chose the latter and was subsequently terminated, there would be no severance.

"Jerry went home, came back in the morning, took the severance offer, signed a release, and quietly and cooperatively left the company."

"That's great," I said.

"I agree," Mary said. "But you know what's probably the best thing?"

"What?"

"It's how I've interacted with Morton and the managers in his department since our meeting. They now let me know much sooner about employee relations issues. Early knowledge gives HR a lot more flexibility. Also, it's no longer a tug-of-war between HR and management; instead, we collaborate on finding jointly acceptable solutions."

MORAL OF THE STORY

I've met many managers who don't have a high opinion of human resources, and many human resources professionals who don't have a high opinion of management. The complaints sound familiar. From management, it's, "They don't understand our business!" "They slow everything down and overcomplicate things!" "They're the Department of 'No'!"

From human resources, it's, "They don't know how to communicate!" "They keep things from us, wait until the last minute, then they're in panic mode and want immediate action!" "Their documentation stinks, and they blame us!"

However, I've also met many managers who say human resources helps them be more effective in their jobs (and I would consider myself one of these managers). And I've met many human resources professionals who experience a great deal of satisfaction interacting with management.

What distinguishes the collaboration camp from the guerilla warfare camp? This story provides a good illustration. Notice the elements. Morton had a long-time festering employee problem in his department yet never brought it to Mary's attention. He waited until he was in crisis mode with pressure from the CEO to cut costs and anxiety about losing good employees to competitors. Morton wanted immediate action from human resources to relieve his pain.

Mary responded from a strictly human resources perspective. Her first question centered on documentation and what she suspected would fall well short of acceptable. Things went downhill from there. The meeting easily could have ended with each of them renewing their respective memberships in the "I hate human resources!" and the "I hate management!" clubs.

What did I do differently? First, I didn't abandon the human resources role. I simply began by making sure I understood the business case from Morton's perspective.

Readers of "If You Want Engagement, Lead by Listening" will observe the EAR method in action.

Second, I resisted the temptation to jump to a conclusion. Instead, I put the issue of Jerry's termination in a risk analysis context using the checklist.

Third, instead of saying "Here's the answer," I presented options, from high risk to low risk, and explored a risk option in between. This approach allowed Morton to participate in finding a solution that would work for his department and human resources.

Most human resources professionals prefer being coaches to cops yet often feel stuck in the latter role. But this doesn't have to be. If you're a human resources professional, I would encourage you to adopt the approach used in this story, an approach that Mary and many other human resources professionals have made a regular practice. If you're a manager and would like to have a better relationship with your human resources people, I suggest you share this story with them and invite a conversation about it. I predict you'll be pleased with the reaction.

CHAPTER
5

HARASSMENT & BULLYING

THREE HARASSMENT STORY SETS

1. SURPRISE HARASSERS

THE ONE-NIGHT STAND
(Don't Use Email to Describe Your Bodily Malfunctions)

Sheldon and Brenda were field engineers who serviced equipment sold to hospitals and medical clinics around the country. During an extended business trip, Sheldon and Brenda spent a great deal of time together, at the customer site and during meals back at the hotel.

They'd had no prior romantic involvement. However, continuous close proximity plus copious amounts of alcohol on their last evening resulted in their sharing the same hotel room that night.

The next morning, Sheldon beamed in excited contemplation of future such rendezvous. Brenda, by contrast, shuddered with disgust. She made a promise to never again drink alcohol with a coworker.

Fortunately for Brenda, they lived and worked in different states. This enabled her to fend off Sheldon's further advances. In addition, she managed to avoid other out-of-town assignments with him.

But for a common email mistake, the story probably would have ended there.

On the night previously referenced, Sheldon had experienced a temporary lower anatomical malfunction. In an email he sent to Brenda the following day, he included a lengthy explanation of what had occurred, how the problem had been corrected, and why she could have full confidence it would not recur in their future get-togethers.

Brenda's reaction? "Yeeechh!" She immediately deleted the message from her inbox and her trash folder. She resisted the temptation to throw her laptop into a wastebasket.

Sheldon had written his "masculine mea culpa" after clicking "Reply" to an email Brenda sent him earlier about an equipment issue. The subject line said "Repair Macro Assembly-5," which Sheldon didn't change. Of course, his reply addressed repair of a very different sort.

Several months passed without further incident. However, one day Sheldon had an idea. As a methodical engineer, he'd saved and sorted email messages that addressed common maintenance and repair issues on company equipment. Thinking it would be helpful for other field engineers to have them, he batched these messages together. He worked from "Subject" lines as opposed to reading each message.

Once he had his batch together, Sheldon scrolled through his directory, clicking email addresses of each of the other field engineers, as well as trainees, managers, and key customer representatives.

You can probably guess what happened next. "Repair Macro Assembly-5" made the list.

As a field engineer, Brenda was on the recipient list. Once again she saw the "Yeeechh!" message. Even more horrifying, she saw the many email addresses in the "To" and "Cc" lines. These included Brenda's boss, her trainees, coworkers, and key customer contacts.

Brenda said nothing to anyone. Instead, she quietly circulated her resume to other companies in the industry. Two months later, she accepted a position with another company.

The outcome wasn't happy for Sheldon either. In addition to his own mortification at having shared embarrassingly private information with his boss, coworkers, trainees, and customers, the corrective action he received made him ineligible for promotion to section supervisor, a position he desired and for which he'd had the inside track.

CEO SEVERS HIS OWN SEVERANCE PACKAGE
(How Not to Evaluate Your Employees)

The abrasive CEO had so alienated the company's board of directors that it wanted to fire him. However, Donald had an employment agreement that provided for generous severance pay if he were terminated without cause. "Cause" included serious, repeated problematic behavior that went uncorrected following notice and warning; it also included immediate termination for egregious misconduct.

Termination for cause meant the company only had to pay him through his last day of work. Termination without cause meant a severance package totaling over $800,000.

Unfortunately for the board, there was no paper trail establishing notice and warning within the meaning of the contract. Moreover, although Donald's behavior was obnoxious, it did not meet the high threshold of egregious misconduct.

Fortunately for the company, while the executive was out of town on business, it was able to conduct a search of his computer and email.

Game change!

The search revealed an email exchange between the CEO and the president of one of its main customers. Their exchange had veered away from business to an entirely different subject: the "bed-ability" of the company's female employees. Referring to employees by name, the men jocularly debated which women would be more likely to _____, which sexual acts would be most pleasurable with _____, and which combinations of women would provide the greatest thrill.

When the CEO returned from his trip, the president of the board of directors handed him notice of immediate termination for cause. She also handed him a booklet containing the emails in question, along with references to relevant portions of his employment agreement and company policies on computer use and sexual harassment.

Finally, she offered to send a set of these materials directly to the CEO's attorney if he desired.

Following a few feeble shots across the bow from the CEO's attorney, the company settled the dispute by agreeing to forgive a small loan it had made the executive (which it had no intention of collecting) in exchange for a comprehensive waiver and release of all claims.

2. SURPRISE PLAINTIFFS

CBT CECIL
(No Complaint Doesn't Mean No Problem)

My client employed a group of mechanics. All men, they developed a practice that supposedly fostered teamwork and camaraderie. Called "CBT," it can be illustrated as follows:

Hands at his side, Mechanic "A" casually walks by Mechanic "B," seemingly paying no attention to the latter. However, just as A crosses B's path, he snaps his wrist upward, the back of his hand making contact with the underside of a highly sensitive part of B's anatomy.

"Gotcha!"

In other words, CBT stands for "casual ball tap."

CBT had been going on for quite a while without complaint to human resources or management. Evidently, self-help was the norm. If a colleague CBTed you, you CBTed him back.

But for a business downturn, this practice would have probably continued to snap under the radar (sorry). However, faced with the need to reduce the number of mechanics it employed, the company applied its informal, undocumented, and not-always-consistent layoff practice, which resulted in it jettisoning its perceived weakest link—Cecil.

Cecil did not, however, go gently into that good night. Instead, he filed a claim of sexual harassment and retaliation. He alleged that CBT had created a sexually hostile environment, that he had complained to his supervisor who did nothing, and that he was selected for the layoff in retaliation for having complained.

The company's investigation did not support Cecil's claim. His supervisor adamantly denied ever hearing a complaint about CBT from Cecil or anyone else. No other mechanic supported Cecil's claims. By all accounts except his, Cecil was a willing, able, and enthusiastic CBT practitioner.

Nevertheless, there were problematic facts for the defense. These included the supervisor's prior knowledge of CBT and occasional indulgence in it himself, and the lack of documentation of both Cecil's weak performance and the company's "weakest link" layoff policy. As a result, the company decided against taking its chances in court and paid off the claim, costing it nearly $20,000.

SHAMELESS SHEILA
(Sometimes the Biggest Offenders Claim
They're the Most Offended)

Sheila was a server at an Italian restaurant. Tall and attractive, she liked to, as she described it, "buzz the boys' engines." Among other things, she often re-created the Katz's Delicatessen scene from the movie "When Harry Met Sally," embellishing her performance with products from the dairy case.

Sheila was not a terribly good employee. Attendance problems and anger management issues combined to make her a challenge for her bosses. One day, she showed up at work by entering through the restaurant's front glass doors, which faced a busy street in a tourist area.

"Sheila," said her manager, "it's 6:00. You're late."

Sheila responded, "You're wrong. I'm not late. My shift starts at 6:00 and it's 6:00."

"No, Sheila, you're supposed to be ready to serve customers at 6:00. Your uniform is on your arm. There's no way you can get back to the changing area, put on your uniform, and be out here while it's still 6:00."

"Oh yeah? Watch me."

Whereupon, in full view of coworkers, patrons, and outside passersby—who were no longer passing by—Sheila removed her outer clothing, leaving her temporarily clad in bra and panties, and then calmly put on her uniform.

"See," she said. "It's still 6:00 and I'm not late."

"That may be true," said her manager, "but you're fired."

Sheila next went to the EEOC, where she filed a claim, alleging she'd been subjected to a hostile work environment based on unwelcome sexual conduct. She also claimed that the employer's stated reason for termination was pretextual: the real reason was her alleged prior internal harassment complaints (of which no one else had knowledge).

The company figured it had a slam-dunk case but was greatly chagrined to learn that the agency didn't see things its way. Although nobody confused Sheila with Mother Teresa, agency investigators showed more interest in what they called a "sexually charged atmosphere pervading the workplace."

The agency recruited a group of current and former employees who asserted they were also victims of sexual harassment. Faced with the prospect of defending a "pattern and practice" lawsuit, the cost of which alone could bankrupt the company, it chose to settle, making payments to Sheila and the other class members. The total cost hit six figures.

POLAROID POLLY
(A Picture Still Tells a Thousand Words)

Years ago in the predigital age, a client of mine was sued by a former employee who had been fired for performance reasons. Polly claimed, however, that she'd been fired for refusing her boss's sexual advances. Her complaint sought $2.5 million in damages.

The manager, Franklin, denied making sexual advances or that any sexual behavior of any kind had occurred. Under persistent questioning, however, he acknowledged having had an affair with Polly, which he said he had ended before her termination.

Polly and Franklin worked for a property-management company and often traveled to apartment complexes to assess their condition. During these visits, they spent time in empty apartments engaging in distinctly nonwork activity.

Franklin had been extremely reluctant to reveal this information. He explained that he and Polly had gone to great lengths to conceal their affair from others, including their respective spouses.

I asked for evidence that might tip the he-said/she-said scales. Franklin said no such evidence existed, a plausible contention in an era before email, texts, instant messaging, Facebook, etc. Yet I pressed him.

"Wasn't there anything—gifts, cards, notes, anything at all—that might support your version of facts?"

"No, I'm sorry. We were too careful."

I continued probing.

Suddenly, Franklin said, "Wait! I just remembered something."

He pulled open his front desk drawer and started rummaging through its contents.

"Aha!" he cried. "Here it is!"

He produced a fragment of a photograph, no more than half an inch in diameter. It showed a female breast.

"Other than the obvious," I said, "what's this?"

"It's from one of our property visits," he said. "We were fooling around in an empty apartment. I grabbed my Polaroid Instamatic that I use to photograph property conditions and took a quick picture of Polly while she was naked. After the picture printed out from the camera, she grabbed it and began tearing it up.

"But then she said, 'I tell you what. I'll give you something to remember me by.' So she tore off this fragment and handed it to me. I put it in my desk drawer and had forgotten about it until your questions made me remember."

At a subsequent mediation session, in the presence of her attorney and her husband, Polly continued to deny that any form of sexual activity had ever occurred. She scoffed at the notion that there might be evidence to the contrary.

I showed her the picture fragment. Polly studied it.

"Well," she said, "it's a woman's breast, and a very nice one at that." She added with a laugh, "Although I wish it was mine, unfortunately it isn't."

I pointed out what appeared to be a few strands of hair adjacent to the breast, and that they appeared to resemble her hair.

"Wrong again," she said.

I explained my intention to have the photograph blown up and analyzed by experts, and that I planned to file a motion with the court to require an examination of the plaintiff in order to make a proper comparison. The plaintiff, her attorney, and her husband responded derisively, and the mediation concluded unsuccessfully.

A few days later, I received a call from plaintiff's counsel. He said his client had reconsidered her position on settlement. "She has magnanimously opted to make peace, not war."

We soon settled for a small fraction of her original $2.5 million demand. You might say it was a mere fragment.

3. SURPRISE VICTIMS

THE BUSINESS TRIP FROM HELL
(A Complaint-Free Environment Doesn't Mean a Harassment-Free Environment)

Janet was vice president of human resources for a large corporation. She had over 20 years of experience in human resources, had conducted harassment investigations and antiharassment training sessions, and had been in court as a representative of her company in harassment litigation.

Her corporation acquired a company in another state. Joined from the home office by William, a senior operations director, Janet visited the company to help with the transition. Although she had not traveled with William before, they had previously gotten along without incident.

The trip was uneventful until the second evening. After work, Janet and William had dinner at their hotel. The conversation included work topics as well as benign personal ones.

Suddenly William steered the conversation in a new direction. He said, "I have a question to ask you Janet. I know you and your husband have been married for a long time just as I've been married for a long time. My question is: Do you and your husband still . . . you know . . . do it?"

Shocked at the question, Janet initially said nothing. Then she stammered out, "Uh, I'm not sure I understand your question, but all I can say is I think we have a normal marriage."

"That's good," William replied. "Unfortunately for me, that's not the case. A few years after our last child was born, my wife said she was done in the you-know-what department."

Janet thought to herself, "Too much information."

William said, "It gets old doing it with a magazine."

Janet thought to herself, "Way too much information!"

William continued, "You know, Janet, you could do me a great favor given my circumstances. If you and I spent tonight together, no one would ever know."

Janet said, "Uh, I don't think so."

"Oh come on," William said. "You really would be doing me a great favor."

"Uh, I don't think so."

By this point, Janet was acutely uncomfortable, doing her best to avoid looking at William and desperately hoping the server would bring the check.

"Okay then," William said. "How about if you let me see you naked? I think that would probably suffice."

Almost mumbling by this point, with her eyes on her plate, Janet said, "I don't think so."

"Come on Janet!" William said. "Be reasonable. All I need

is a little help. If I bought you a bikini from the hotel gift store, would you put it on and let me look at you in it?"

"I don't think so."

"Final offer," William said. "Let me see one breast. Okay? Just one."

After this elicited the same response from Janet, William gave up this line of questioning. Janet soon excused herself from the table, saying she wasn't feeling well. She went up to her hotel room, making sure she hadn't been followed. Once in her room, she quickly double locked the door and put up the chain. Then she collapsed on the bed.

For the remainder of the trip and thereafter, Janet did everything she could to maintain distance between herself and William. Fortunately, he resigned a few months after this incident and left the company.

"DUMB BEANER"
(The Object of Offensive Behavior Isn't Necessarily the One Offended)

The trucking company employed 17 drivers: 15 Anglo Americans and 2 Mexican Americans. One of the Mexican American employees had a habit of poking fun at his own national origin. If he made a mistake, he'd say, "Oh, I'm just a dumb beaner." He made other comments invoking negative stereotypes of Mexicans.

Perceiving no sense of discomfort, several Anglo employees joined in the "beaner" banter. Thanks to the company's dispatch and radio systems, these comments had a wide circulation.

No one complained. No one reported observing signs of distress.

However, as I mentioned, the company employed two Mexican American drivers. The other driver, Joseph, took pride in his country of origin. He hated these comments. Yet he said and showed nothing. He didn't want to get people mad at him or be perceived as weak. So as best he could, he continued to stomach the anti-Mexican jocularity.

Bottling up his emotions wasn't healthy. Joseph increasingly felt uncomfortable, isolated, and helpless.

Eventually things reached the boiling point, and the lid came off.

An inspection revealed a minor problem with Joseph's truck, something he'd overlooked. Word got around to the other drivers. In the break room, a couple of Anglo drivers started teasing him. One said, "I guess we have more than one dumb beaner around here." The other drivers laughed.

Joseph said nothing. After a sleepless night, he did not report to work the next day. Nor the next one, nor the next. No one in management contacted him. Instead, the company sent him a termination notice based on "job abandonment."

Joseph responded by engaging the services of a noted civil rights attorney, and he soon asserted claims of harassment, retaliation, and constructive discharge, alleging that his working environment had become so toxic, he was compelled to quit.

Managers had been aware of the anti-Mexican comments but had done nothing to stop them. When I asked why, their responses included faulting Joseph. "We had no idea there was a problem. If Joseph was bothered by the talk, why didn't he let us know?"

One manager said, "When the first Mexican guy started making those beaner comments, I thought about telling him to knock it off. But I figured it might be risky for a white guy like me to tell a Mexican not to say stuff about Mexicans. So I let it go."

I asked, "Why did no one contact Joseph after he was a no-show?"

A manager answered, "I had a hunch he was upset, but it's the driver's responsibility to show up to work, not ours. If he had a complaint, he needed to tell us. Besides, Joseph wasn't that great of a driver anyway."

After nearly five years of legal proceedings, the company finally settled Joseph's claim. Total cost to the company (not including lost labor hours and productivity) was in the six figures.

LET'S SETTLE THIS CASE!
(Employees Sometimes Leave Jobs for
Unexpected Reasons)

Monica worked as an electrical engineer in an overwhelmingly male environment. After working for her company for a little over two years, she accepted a position with a competitor. Her former employer responded by suing her and her new employer, alleging that her new employment violated a noncompete agreement she'd signed.

The legal battle raged for months. I represented Monica and her current employer. When I first interviewed her in preparing our defense, she told me she left her former employer "because it was a better career opportunity for me, the pay and benefits were superior and my commute time less." No other reasons were given.

However, during the discovery process, I learned some things about her former supervisor that made me suspicious. This prompted me to sit down with Monica again to go over why she left. She repeated the reasons she'd given me before. However, this time I kept probing, "Was there anything else? Was there anything about your former supervisor that influenced your decision? Even if you're reluctant to share this information, it's important I know the full facts before we go to trial."

Monica sighed and said, "The reasons I gave you are true. It is a better career opportunity, the pay is better, and the commute shorter. However, I didn't tell you what got me looking for another job in the first place. It was my supervisor."

She then recounted sexually offensive behavior, which included her supervisor making crude comments, inappropriate touching, and propositions. Monica had attempted to discourage this behavior but without success. Rather than go to human resources or senior management, she chose to look for another job.

Armed with this new information, I contacted opposing counsel and said the case was about to go in a direction that would probably not be good for his client. I suggested he investigate the new facts, including the supervisor's behavior toward other women. If he found substance in them, his client might want to rethink its scorched-earth-litigation position.

About a week later, I got a call. "I think we can reach a deal," opposing counsel said. We quickly worked out terms, which included Monica's former employer dropping all claims in exchange for her agreeing not to disclose trade secret information and agreeing not to bring a countersuit for sexual harassment. Monica was able to keep her job and move on with her life.

Case closed.

MORAL OF THE STORY

SURPRISE HARASSERS. Sheldon and Donald are classic examples of what I call the surprise harasser. These are people who engage in workplace sexual behavior without ever thinking that what they're doing is inappropriate or might be hurtful to others. They're not so much malevolent as they're misguided. They make erroneous assumptions about how welcome their behavior is or about its limited scope or impact. They are therefore surprised when their behavior is deemed harassing.

In 25 years of harassment litigation, I dealt with some true predators. However, I can tell you that most of the people whose actions caused harassment trouble fell into the surprise harasser category. They weren't out to hurt anyone yet unwittingly did so, including themselves.

SURPRISE PLAINTIFFS. Cecil, Sheila and Polly are examples of what I call surprise plaintiffs, employees who engage in the very behavior they later use against their employers. What causes the shift? Typically, it's when something happens they don't like, such as discipline or discharge. Suddenly, they view behavior of the type in which they themselves engaged as having created a hostile environment *for them.* Surprise plaintiffs typically also claim they had complained about their environment to someone in management or human resources; this gives them a basis to claim the disciplinary action against them is unlawful retaliation. Essentially, it's the best-defense-is-a-good-offense stance.

I'm not saying most plaintiffs fall into this category. Yet enough of them do that it behooves management to be aware of the phenomenon. Typically, management learns this the hard way. It receives an unpleasant surprise. The person they thought least likely to complain is now making a formal complaint in the U.S. legal system.

SURPRISE VICTIMS. Janet, Joseph, and Monica (as well as Brenda in one of the "Surprise Harassers" stories) fall in the category of surprise victims, people who don't express their discomfort even though they feel it. I believe most harassment victims fall into this category. No matter what your policy says or how many training classes you conduct, they won't say anything. Fear of conflict, ostracism, retaliation, or embarrassment, plus sometimes self-blame and denial, can cause the very people the law is designed to protect to distance themselves from its protections.

Consider Janet, the vice president of human resources. What action did she take on her own behalf? I was the first person she ever told her story to, and then only because I was about to conduct antiharassment classes at her company. I explained the surprise-victim phenomenon and told her I wanted to talk about it in the classes. Would she be okay with my doing so? Her response: "I'm one of those surprise victims."

Even if no claim is filed, employers and employees pay a price for the surprise-victim phenomenon. Unlike Joseph, who left and sued after reaching the breaking point, Monica found other employment, as did Brenda. Had William remained employed, Janet probably would have left as well. For organizations with this problem, the cost may be hidden, but it's still quite steep.

THE SOLUTION: ADOPT SPEED LIMIT 55

In the wake of the 1970s Arab oil embargo, Congress passed a law capping all state and federal speed limits at 55 mph. Sustained public outcry against this law eventually resulted in its repeal. (You may recall a certain rock 'n' roll protest song from the early 1980s by the "Red Rocker" Sammy Hagar, "I Can't Drive 55.")

I use Speed Limit 55 as a symbol of harassment prevention. The 65, 70, and 75 mph speed limits we have on today's roads are like today's antiharassment laws. You can go pretty fast.

Objectionable workplace behavior relating to sex, race, or other conditions doesn't necessarily violate the law, even if it offends someone. Courts require additional elements of proof. The conduct must be "unwelcome" and "pervasive" or "severe." It must pass a subjective and objective test of "abusive working environment."

By contrast, Speed Limit 55 moves away from the legal standard. The issue is not whether the behavior is "pervasive," "severe," or meets the "abusive" test. It's not even whether the behavior is "unwelcome." Rather, it's whether the behavior is in any way sexual, racial, religious, or otherwise related to the categories designated by law as protected. If so, it doesn't belong in the workplace, regardless of whether or not someone has complained or whether or not someone is offended. The behavior simply stays out.

Speed Limit 55 protects surprise harassers from themselves. They can no longer rely on their assumptions that their behavior is okay because no one has complained or seems offended. It protects employers from surprise plaintiffs who can no longer play the best-defense-is-a-good-offense card. And it protects surprise victims by fostering an environment where surprise harassers aren't running around distressing people who don't complain.

Employees who exceed Speed Limit 55 may not be exceeding the legal speed limit. However, as these stories show, they're on a slippery slope. The path may start out level, but it begins to change. Without being aware, the person increasingly picks up speed. Soon the edge of the cliff appears, but the person can't stop in time. Over the cliff he or she goes, bringing the employer along for the ride—and the crash.

Stay off the slippery slope. Adopt Speed Limit 55.

THE BULLY BOSS
("Equal Opportunity Offender" Is No Defense)

Rocky stood six feet five inches and had a barrel chest and a short fuse. He was the superintendent of a construction site, and his vocabulary was small. Most words had four letters, which he used with vigor. Rocky motivated employees primarily through fear.

One of Rocky's employees, Lee, was African American. A slender, sensitive man, Lee had a difficult time coping with Rocky. Over time, he began to suffer from anxiety, sleeplessness, and other health-related problems, which he felt were due to his work environment.

One day, Rocky got upset with Lee. He got within inches of Lee's face, stared down at him, eyes hard, and pointed a thick finger in his face: "What the #$@!%&'s the matter with you? You worthless piece of #$@!%&*! I ought to knock the #$@!%&* out of you!"

That was the last straw. Lee quit and filed harassment claims with federal and state agencies. He alleged that he had been subjected to a hostile environment based on race and that conditions got so bad he was compelled to quit, meaning in the law he'd been "constructively discharged."

My investigation of Lee's claim revealed no evidence to support the claim that Rocky mistreated him because of his race, an essential element of the harassment claim. In fact, Rocky showed remarkable evenhandedness in his treatment of employees of all races and ethnicities. Rocky was the true equal opportunity offender. He treated everyone equally horribly.

We soon settled Lee's claim for a small amount of money. However, that was not the end of the story.

My investigation also revealed that Rocky's methods had created an environment where employees kept their heads down and mouths shut. Hear no evil, see no evil was the order of the day. One employee had recently hurt his knee and another had strained his back in on-the-job injuries. However, both chose not to report their injuries from fear of Rocky's reaction.

On one occasion, a small group of employees had reported to Rocky an unsafe work condition. He responded by haranguing them: "What the hell is the matter with you people?! Are you that stupid?! I'm surrounded by #$@!%&* morons!"

Word of this tongue-lashing got around, which effectively eliminated the possibility that a future safety problem would be reported to management. During my investigation of Lee's claim, I learned that there was a problem at the work site that presented a potentially deadly hazard. In addition to the threat to employee safety, if this condition were discovered during a government inspection, the plant would have been shut down.

When I shared this information with senior leaders, they were shocked. "Wow, we had no idea this kind of thing was going on! No one said anything, and Rocky has certainly never acted that way in our presence. Around us, he's been a perfect gentleman."

Nevertheless, based on the overwhelming evidence of Rocky's misconduct, senior leadership decided to fire him.

Rocky's response: "You can't do this to me! I didn't discriminate against anybody! Hell, I'm married to a Mexican woman!"

Rocky's lawyer sent a letter to the company threatening a lawsuit. Although we considered the claim baseless, the company agreed to give Rocky six months' severance pay, in large part because company employees were fearful of what Rocky might do to them for "ratting him out." We conditioned settlement payments on Rocky's having no further contact with anyone in the company outside of the human resources director and that the money would be paid over time to ensure good behavior.

Rocky took the money and went away quietly. A few years

later, we learned that he had landed a management job in another state but had subsequently been fired after punching an employee.

This story highlights two important points. The first is that the Speed Limit 55 concept discussed in the harassment stories applies here too. It means focusing on company values regarding the kind of workplace behavior that's acceptable, not primarily on legal compliance.

This client had a conventional antiharassment policy that listed legally protected classes and prohibited discrimination and harassment based on them. Company training followed the same lines. This enabled Rocky to argue that he was still policy compliant.

Had the company centered its efforts on a working environment where everyone is treated with dignity, respect, and professionalism at all times, Rocky's argument would have lost its teeth. Productivity would have increased. Workplace injuries and hazards would have been dealt with promptly and properly. And Lee would probably still be working there.

Bullies who aren't racists or sexists are still bullies. Don't tolerate them.

The second point is the mistake many senior executives make. They assume that how managers treat them is how they treat their subordinates. Yet in my career, I've encountered many "kiss-up, kick-down" managers. Do you employ any? Would you know if you did?

As this story indicates, don't expect your employees to come forward on their own if they have an abusive boss. And if you're in senior leadership, don't assume you'll see the warning signs if a problem exists. Make it a point to find out if your organization employs any Rockys.

CHAPTER
6

CONFLICT RESOLUTION

PREVENTING THE SHOOTOUT AT THE NOT-OK CORRAL (When Faced with a Contentious Meeting, Apply the Monks Technique)

The board of directors had two armed camps: camp one—fire the CEO; camp two—retain the CEO. The upcoming board meeting would decide his fate. With lines drawn and sides taken, tensions were high. Trouble brewed.

The board brought me in to facilitate the meeting. As everyone took seats around the conference-room table, board members sat according to the side of the issue they were on. Small talk was very small, and strained.

I began the meeting by stating the issue before them, and the importance of how they addressed and resolved it. I then said, "Let me share a story about a European monastery that had a problem. When the monks got together to discuss scripture, the exchanges often got out of hand. Debates would become heated, personal, and leave wounds.

"As a result, the monastery established a rule. Whenever one monk disagreed with another, he could only do so if he confirmed with the other monk the position that he was about to dispute.

"Let's say, for example, we're monks at that monastery, and the topic is the expulsion from the Garden of Eden."

I looked at one of the board members and said, "Let's say Jim here asserts that it's Eve's fault."

I looked at another board member and said, "Gabby vehemently disagrees with Jim's view. She thinks it's Adam's fault. Gabby's free to express her disagreement however she wishes so long as she first confirms with Jim his view."

I continued. "Now let's say that after Gabby finishes stating her position, Jim wants to return fire. He likewise can do so provided he first confirms Gabby's position with her."

I looked at another board member and said, "Now let's say Erica disagrees with both Jim and Gabby. She thinks it's the serpent. Again, Erica has the freedom to do so provided she first confirms with each of them the views she's about to disagree with."

At that point, a prominent and outspoken board member frowned and raised his hand. "Yes?" I said.

"I have a problem with your rule Jathan. I've got other things to do after this meeting. If we do all this confirming about what we disagree with, we'll waste a lot of time. I don't have all night!"

"I agree with you," I said. "We don't want to waste time, and we don't want to be here all night. However, I believe the Monks Technique will actually prevent those things from happening. I also think it will enable the board to make a decision in the best overall interest of the company, drawing on the experience and insights of everyone here. And it will help the board function cohesively after this meeting. That includes the board members whose position prevails tonight and those whose position does not."

"But I tell you what," I added. "If the technique starts to bog us down, we'll abandon it."

The meeting proceeded. Results? The tension in the room left almost immediately. No angry outbursts. No ad hominem arguments. Instead, the exchanges were thoughtful, respectful, and substantive.

Although the board didn't always follow the technique religiously (pardon the pun), there was enough confirming and clarifying that all sides of the issue were fairly vetted, including the pros and cons of letting go or retaining the CEO, the steps that would need to be taken in each scenario, and how the board would work together after the meeting.

Score one for the monks.

MORAL OF THE STORY

Readers of "If You Want Engagement, Lead by Listening" will observe that the Monks Technique is a variation of the EAR listening method. Instead of starting with the "E," for "explore," you begin with the "A," for "acknowledge." If the other person confirms your understanding, you move to the "R"—your substantive "response."

If the other person says, "No, that's not my position," you move back to "E"—"explore"—using open-ended questions such as, "What did I miss?"

Contrary to the one board member's fear of prolonging the meeting, the Monks Technique did the opposite. It promoted efficiency. No erroneous assumptions were made. How many times have you experienced or participated in an argument where people made assumptions about each other, their positions, views, motives, etc., that were vigorously denied as accurate? You then had a battle over what the person's position was, as opposed to its merits.

In addition, the technique creates an environment of respect, which happens naturally when people really listen to each other. Instead of erroneous assumptions heating up the debate, emotions cool, enabling people to focus on substance.

The Monks Technique works not only in meetings but in any encounter where you can anticipate strong disagreement. You don't have to announce it or propose it as a rule of discussion as I did with the board of directors. The main point is to follow the sequence, confirming your understanding of the other side's position before stating yours.

One of my favorite examples comes from a manager who learned this technique at my workshop and applied it later that day at his son's school. His son Johnny was in a special needs program. A dispute had arisen between Johnny's parents and school officials regarding the boy's treatment. The parents felt the school was not doing what it was morally and legally obligated to do for their son, whereas school officials felt the parents were in denial. A meeting had been scheduled between the parents, the school principal, and the head of the special needs program.

The manager explained, "As my wife and I walked into the school, I could see she was gearing herself up for battle. So I asked her if it would be okay if I spoke first. She said okay.

"We sat down on one side of the table, and the school principal and the program head sat down on the other. I said, 'Before we get going, I want to be sure I fully understand the school's position on Johnny.' I then summarized it as best I could from their perspective, making the case for them as if I were in their shoes.

"When I finished, I asked them, 'Have I summarized your position accurately?' They said, 'Not entirely.' To my surprise, they clarified their position in a way that made it closer to and more supportive of our side of the issue.

"We ended the meeting with a fully agreed game plan for Johnny. My wife, who'd been ready to declare war, instead walked around the table and hugged the two school officials."

The Monks Technique: Give it a try.

A MIDNIGHT ENCOUNTER AT A PORTLAND PUB
(Instead of Fight or Flight, Try Verbal Aikido)

Divided by the Willamette River and Burnside Street, Portland, Oregon, is known by its four quadrants: Northeast,

Northwest, Southeast, and Southwest. On a Friday night following a play my friend and I had attended at an out-of-the-way theater in the Northeast quadrant, we stopped for a beer at a nearby pub.

Shortly before midnight, we got up to leave. A considerably younger and bigger man accosted us. Although well dressed, he was, as the Brits say, clearly in his cups.

Thrusting his face in mine, he said harshly, "What are you two talking about?!"

Although my danger light lit up, I remained calm. I didn't back away or counter his aggression. Instead, I said, "I don't know—the usual: sports, politics. Why do you ask?"

"You're not from around here!" he responded. "What quadrant are you from?"

"Quadrant?" I said. "What do you mean? Quadrant of the universe? Quadrant of the planet?"

"No!" he said, "Portland. I'm from Northeast, and I haven't been shot!"

Before I could respond, the man again said, "I'm from Northeast, and I haven't been shot!"

"That reminds me of a quote from Winston Churchill," I said.

"I don't like Churchill!"

"Yes, but you might like this quote: 'Nothing is so exhilarating as to be shot at, without result.'"

He paused, evidently pondering the quotation.

I said again, "Nothing is so exhilarating as to be shot at, without result."

The man's posture changed, his shoulders and face relaxed. In a tone no longer harsh, he said, "I do like that quote. I really do."

He extended his hand. I took it. We briefly exchanged small talk while over my shoulder, I gave my friend a look that said, "Time to gooooo." We left the pub without further incident.

Whew!

Many years ago, I studied karate. We drilled endlessly on block-strike techniques. The attacker strikes, you block the attack and strike the attacker. Notwithstanding her repeated admonition that "the best fight is the one you avoid," our sensei had us do pushups on the hardwood dojo floor—on our knuckles. This was to harden the striking surface of our fists, which would improve our ability to break boards and, at least theoretically, bones.

Many years ago, a Japanese martial arts expert, Morihei Ueshiba, departed from conventional martial arts because even if intended as defensive, they trained actions that could result in injury or death to attackers. Ueshiba developed a martial art form called aikido designed to defend against attack without causing injury to anyone.

In aikido, when the attack comes, instead of block-strike, you blend with the attacker and flow with the person's energy. You turn with the attacker and see what the attacker sees. While conserving your energy and maintaining your balance, you lead the attacker to a position where the person can't hurt you, and you don't inflict injury either.

Aikido can be applied to verbal attacks. Let's say you present an idea in a meeting and someone responds, "That's the stupidest idea I ever heard!" According to neuroscience, that comment will light up the threat-recognition area of your brain just as a physical threat would.

You could go into flight mode: become quiet, withdrawn or placating, or literally flee the meeting. Or you could go into block-strike fight mode: "My idea is not stupid!" (block) "You're stupid!" (strike)

Or you could engage, blend, and flow with the attack by becoming curious and genuinely inquisitive. "Oh really, the stupidest ever. What specifically makes it so stupid?" Or if you want to work a little humor in, you could say, "Oh really, the stupidest ever. What's No. 2?"

The point is to ask open-ended questions that draw out your attacker in ways the person will probably not anticipate. The attacker continues to expend energy and struggles to stay balanced while you stay relaxed and centered. Often what the attacker says in response to your questions will give you new openings to settle things down and find a resolution point. "So if I understand you, what makes my idea stupid is 'X.' If we can resolve 'X,' then my idea is no longer stupid, is that right?"

In my Portland pub encounter, without thinking about it, I went into aikido mode. I engaged and blended with the man's hostile words. He opened with a question. I responded with a question. He mentioned quadrants. So did I. He mentioned the concept of being shot. So did I. Finally, with the Churchill quote, we found common ground, and the hostility ended.

I'll confess I didn't know where any of this was going, and it remained a distinct possibility that I would be served a knuckle sandwich. Yet I kept probing, blending, flowing, and channeling until we ended up where he was no longer hostile. The key was to get into an aikido frame of mind. That enabled me to engage without fight or flight.

The next time a verbal attack comes your way, don't freeze up and don't return fire. Instead, look calmly at your attacker. Blend with the attack—flow with and channel the attacker's energy to where the anger dissipates and the two of you can agree, or reasonably agree to disagree.

I'LL DO IT WITH ANYBODY BUT MONIQUE!
(To End a Feud, Apply the Triple Two)

After my presentation, the young woman approached cautiously. "Excuse me," Susan said. "May I ask you a question?"

"Sure," I said.

"I have a difficult situation at work and wonder if what you call the Triple Two might help."

"What's the situation?" I asked.

"I work in our customer service department. There's a process where I have to coordinate with three people in other departments. However, we don't function well. Cooperation is poor, which affects the work and causes a lot of stress. Unfortunately, management has been no help.

"The problem's not getting better; it's getting worse. I'm starting to think I need to find another job."

I said, "Perhaps something like the Triple Two would be helpful. What do you think about going to each of them separately, identifying the problem, and asking them what two things you could start doing that would help, two things you could stop doing that are currently getting in the way, and two things you should continue doing because they add value?"

Susan thought for a moment and said, "I can see doing this with Jane and Elizabeth but not with Monique."

"Why not Monique?"

"Because she's horrible! I don't dare make myself vulnerable. If I ask her what I should stop doing, she'll probably say, 'Breathing!'"

I laughed and said, "I suppose there's a chance of that, but I don't think it's likely. I predict a very different response, that Monique responds favorably."

Susan looked at me skeptically, so I said, "You see, you and Monique actually have a lot in common."

"No we don't! I have nothing in common with her!"

"Yes you do," I replied with a smile. "You both have in

common the fact that you make each other miserable, and that you undermine each other's job satisfaction and sense of accomplishment. And you both have in common the enormous payoff if someone breaks the current pattern of behavior. That's what I predict the Triple Two will do.

"And besides," I added with a chuckle. "If she tells you to stop breathing, you can always ask her to show you how."

Susan took my advice and later shared the results with me. Monique not only permitted Susan to draw oxygen, she offered concrete suggestions to improve their situation. To Susan's great surprise, Monique even offered Susan the opportunity to Triple Two her.

Susan had similar results with Jane and Elizabeth. Subsequently, all four women met and worked out a successful interdepartmental game plan.

Susan's stress level went way down while her sense of job satisfaction went way up.

And she breathed easy.

MORAL OF THE STORY

The Triple Two technique involves asking three questions that call for two responses each:

1. What two things should I start doing?
2. What two things should I stop doing?
3. What two things should I continue to do?

The technique focuses on specific behavior. "Start" and "stop" identify obstacles that are often hidden as well as opportunities that are being neglected. "Continue" preserves what is working. There's no magic to the number two; it just means the other party isn't limited to a single response.

For long-standing or structural conflicts with recurring flash points, the Triple Two is a great tool to change the status quo. It does mean making yourself vulnerable since you're asking someone you don't yet trust what you should start/stop/continue, not what the other person should start/stop/continue. The "stop breathing" response is a possibility. However, in my experience, it's not been the reality. A great many Susans have been pleasantly surprised when their opponent didn't use the opening to attack but instead accepted their invitation to constructive problem solving.

There are four reasons why other people aren't likely to respond in the negative way you might fear:

1. As I explained to Susan, chances are they are experiencing as much pain or frustration as you are and will recognize your opening as a way out.
2. Human beings are wired with a reciprocity gene. When you open yourself up to them, there's a natural inclination to reciprocate, giving you the opportunity to Triple Two them while they're receptive.
3. The "continue" part ensures there will be something positive in the message.

4. You're not asking them for their overall opinion, evaluation, or characterization of you as a person, the kinds of topics that get the blood boiling. Instead, you're simply seeking to identify specific behaviors in a solution-oriented context.

I've used and coached the Triple Two to resolve individual, team, and interdepartmental conflicts, and it has worked quite well in many settings. The key is that no one judges anyone else. Attention and effort remain focused on how to make things work.

BONUS MORAL OF THE STORY

The Triple Two has applications beyond conflict resolution. One of the best is in performance reviews. When used by the supervisor, it creates a permission-to-speak-freely environment in which the employee says what the supervisor could start doing, stop doing, and continue doing that would help the employee succeed in meeting the supervisor's expectations. Many employers have built the Triple Two into their performance review process. Some have jettisoned forms, categories, and ratings and instead created a process that combines the Star Profile ("Beating the Coin Toss"), a mutual Triple Two, and the Same Day Summary ("Texas Wes"). The idea is to promote collaborative goal setting and goal seeking versus the teacher's-report-card form of feedback described in "Performance Review Follies."

Employees have used the Triple Two to manage up, such as with bosses who tend to undercommunicate (leaving employees guessing about expectations), or over-communicate (i.e., micromanage). Periodically asking the boss to Triple Two you while making it clear the purpose is "so that I can help you achieve your goals" does two things:

1. It gives you valuable information about the boss's priorities.
2. It signals the boss that you're an employee who can be trusted.

I've experienced too many success stories to overstate the value of this tool. It's as powerful as it is simple. So when it comes to getting feedback from others, stop your current practice, start using the Triple Two, and once you do, be sure to continue.

AN APOLOGY TRILOGY

APOLOGY #1: "Buddy Bill's Bar & Babes"
(An Apology Creates a Fresh Offense)

At one of its properties, a company employed a leasing agent, Jill. She had a lengthy disciplinary history. In addition to performance and attendance problems, she'd twice been sent home for wearing overly revealing clothing.

One day at work, Jill told a group of coworkers that she had accepted a job working weekends at "Buddy Bill's Bar & Babes." As the name implies, Buddy Bill's featured exotic women dancers.

A maintenance worker, Otis, asked her, "Will you strip?"

Jill did not reply. Instead she went to the property manager and complained. "Otis just humiliated me in front of my coworkers!"

"What happened?" the property manager asked.

"He asked me to take off my clothes right there in the break room!" Jill replied. "I've been sexually harassed!"

The property manager confronted Otis. "Did you ask Jill to take off her clothes?"

"No!" Otis replied. "I asked her what job she would be doing at Buddy Bill's."

"I think there's been a misunderstanding," the manager said. "I suggest you go and apologize to her."

Otis agreed. He went to Jill and said, "I'm sorry if I offended you with my comment about stripping."

After a pause, he added, "But you misunderstood. I was talking about your job at Buddy Bill's." Looking Jill up and down, Otis said, "I probably didn't need to ask. It's pretty obvious you won't be working the cash register."

Apology accepted?

Jill went back to the property manager and demanded that Otis be fired, which the manager declined to do, writing Otis up instead. There were no further incidents between Otis and Jill.

However, Jill's performance problems continued. After she misapplied several rent payments, the manager put her on final-warning status. Jill responded by saying, "I'm being picked on! It's not my fault!"

Two weeks later, Jill got into a shouting match with one of the residents. For the property manager, this was the last straw. She fired Jill.

Jill responded by filing claims of sexual harassment and retaliation, which the company successfully defended, but only after much time and money had been spent.

APOLOGY #2: "Your Presidency Has Been a Failure" (An Insincere Apology Is Worse Than No Apology)

While serving as president of a nonprofit organization, I attended a social function for organization members. As I pleasantly conversed with several members over wine, cheese, and vegetables, a member, Roderick, approached. In the presence of the others, he said, "You know, Jathan, your presidency has been a failure."

Stunned, I said nothing. The other members looked down at their plates of food.

Roderick added, "I just thought you'd like to know," and wandered off.

I went home that night and told my wife. She knew Roderick's wife. An exchange between wives produced a phone call from Roderick.

"I understand you're upset with my comment at the social," he said, "Let's have lunch and talk about it."

The following week, we met outside a restaurant. I was in a suit. Roderick pointed at my tie.

"Where did you get that from?" he said, his voice dripping sarcasm.

"Why do you ask?" I replied.

"So I know where not to shop!" (So much for breaking the ice.)

We went inside, sat down, and ordered our meals.

Roderick got down to business. "I'm sorry if my comment offended you. But you misunderstood me. You see, I wasn't saying that you were a personal failure, only that your presidency was. I was simply pointing out that in an organization as functionally screwed up as this one is, any president would fail. Jathan, you need to understand. There's an important distinction between individual failure and collective failure."

I thanked Roderick for his clarification, although the look on my face should have told him my gratitude wasn't sincere.

The server put the check on the table. I stared at it. Roderick stared at it.

"I'll get it," I said. I reached for the check, slowly.

"Let's split it," Roderick said.

I shook my head. "No, I insist. This experience has been worth it."

When I got home that evening, I told my wife what happened. At a loss for words but sweet soul that she is, she pointed at my tie and said, "I really like it!"

APOLOGY #3: Even a Lawyer Can Apologize!
(When Apologizing, Use the MIDAS Touch)

Early one Monday morning when I managed my law firm's Portland and Seattle offices, I got a call from Rich, a powerful partner in the firm's Washington, D.C., office. Rich was not happy.

"Jathan," he said in an agitated tone, "I have a complaint to make about a partner in one of your offices."

"What is it?" I asked.

Rich explained that Natalie had dropped the ball on an assignment, which angered the client's CEO. Rich added, "This is a highly important and lucrative client for our firm. Natalie has jeopardized this relationship!"

After questioning Rich further, I learned what really infuriated him. After the problem arose, Rich requested an explanation from Natalie. She responded in an email. The first part of her message acknowledged dropping the ball. The second part listed mistakes others had made, including Rich and the CEO. The message concluded, "In any event, the client's substantive position was not adversely affected."

Natalie's "apology" prompted Rich to call me and say, "I'm prepared to take my complaint directly to the board of directors!"

I promised Rich I'd look into it. I went to Natalie and shared my conversation with Rich. Natalie became defensive. "How dare he complain to you! If he has an issue with me, he should call me, not you!"

She added, "I think I'm being scapegoated here. Sure, I

could have handled things better. However, other mistakes were made including by Rich and the client's CEO. It's unfair to pin the blame on me. I have a good mind to call Rich right now and let him know exactly what I think!"

I said, "Okay, Natalie. Call Rich. Give him a piece of your mind. And let's see how that plays out. Tell me if you disagree, but here's what I see happening. You call Rich and let him know how upset you are that he contacted me instead of you, and that you're being scapegoated. What's the likelihood Rich escalates this issue to the board of directors? My guess is 100 percent.

"So let's say the issue goes to the board. What's its likely reaction? Remember that you've acknowledged that some fault lies with you. How will you look? Think about who's on the board. Aren't these the business rainmakers you rely on to supply you with work? How will this play out in terms of your maintaining their confidence in you and their continuing as an important source of your work?

"Oh," said Natalie. "I see what you mean. What should I do?"

"How about apologizing to Rich?," I asked. "Only this time, not through email. Make it a real-time telephone conversation. In fact, if you weren't so far apart geographically, I'd say face to face. Here's a method to use, which I call the MIDAS Touch apology:

> ▶ **"M" is for "Mistake."** Acknowledge to Rich the mistake you made, the ball you dropped, and the poorly worded email that inflamed the situation.

▸ **"I" is for "Injury."** Instead of focusing on the fact the client wasn't hurt, focus on the injury caused in making the CEO mad and causing Rich a great deal of anxiety and stress.

▸ **"D" is for "Differently."** This is what you will do differently going forward. You told me earlier that you made an adjustment to your calendaring system because of this incident. Tell Rich that.

▸ **"A" is for "Amends."** Do something to make amends—perhaps offer to contact the client directly to apologize. Or perhaps you could find out Rich's favorite restaurant in D.C., to which you'll provide your credit card information so that Rich and his wife can dine out on you. The idea is take concrete action to show that you really want to heal things.

▸ **"S" is for "Stop."** After you finish saying the first four parts, stop talking. Don't say another word. Let Rich do the talking."

I wrote "MIDAS" on a sticky note and handed it to Natalie. "When you have that conversation with Rich," I said, "make sure you have this sticky note in the palm of your hand. Trust me, it will help."

Two days later, Natalie came by my office. "Jathan," she said, "I just got off the phone with Rich."

"What happened?" I asked.

"I followed the MIDAS Touch approach. I got to the 'S' and stopped talking. And then the most amazing thing happened."

"What?" I asked.

"Rich said the things I was dying to say but didn't—that other people dropped balls including himself and the client, and that fortunately the client wasn't hurt."

"That's great," I said.

Natalie continued. "Rich said that things have been patched up with the client, that he's no longer worried about the relationship, and that he will continue to use me for legal matters in our region."

"That's wonderful," I said. "A happy ending."

Natalie turned to leave my office, then swiveled around and said, "One more thing. I have to admit that when I spoke to Rich, if I didn't have the sticky note in the palm of my hand, I would've blown it. I got to the 'S' but didn't want to stop! But I looked at the note and stopped talking. That's when things turned positive."

MORAL OF THE STORY

These three stories show the impact of apologies, positive and negative. On the one hand, they can heal rifts and restore relationships. On the other, they can make the original offense worse. Perhaps that's why we don't apologize as often as we should: We've had too much experience with apologies backfiring.

I came up with the MIDAS acronym as a form of self-discipline. It prevents us from letting our "buts" get in the way. The first element admits wrongdoing—you screwed up. The second element acknowledges that you caused damage—don't qualify it with "if." The third element demonstrates your sincerity—it's not a phony apology. The fourth element means you truly care about restoring the relationship. The fifth element, often the hardest of all, means resisting the temptation to explain yourself—instead, hit the self-mute button.

Since I began teaching and coaching the MIDAS Touch, I've heard numerous success stories. Rifts healed, relationships restored, new paths carved. In addition to work experiences, there have been personal ones, including employees who've shared with me that a MIDAS Touch apology changed a relationship trajectory from the rocks to the chapel.

Although I am entirely over the incident with Roderick in "Your Presidency Has Been a Failure," for your edification, I will apply the MIDAS Touch formula to his "apology."

In his speech to me, did Roderick admit making a "Mistake"? Let me know if you heard one; I certainly didn't.

What about "Injury"? Recall his "if my comment offended you." *If* I was offended? Did he think I was faking it? Also, was he suggesting his "comment" did the offending, not him? So I should be mad at the comment and not at him?

How about "Differently"—did anything suggest Roderick wouldn't repeat his behavior in similar circumstances? I know where my betting money is.

What about "Amends"? Come on Roderick—pick up the check.

Lastly, instead of "Stop," Roderick treated me to a lecture on the fine distinctions between individual failure and collective failure. Gee thanks for the education.

As I said, I am entirely over this incident. Entirely.

BONUS MORAL OF THE STORIES

Readers of "A Midnight Encounter at a Portland Pub" will observe an example of Verbal Aikido in my initial exchange with Natalie. Recall her threat to call Rich and give him a piece of her mind. Although I thought this a horrid idea, I didn't say so. Instead, I turned with her in that direction. Through questions about how things would likely play out, I helped her see that doing so would not be in her own best interest.

In addition, readers of "Discharge from Four Doors Down" will see another example of how not communicating directly adds insult to injury. Instead of a real-time conversation with Rich on a sensitive subject, Natalie sent him an email, which only fueled the fire. I made sure she didn't repeat that mistake.

CHAPTER
7

STOPPING PROBLEMS
BEFORE THEY START

AUTOPSY OF A TERMINAL EMPLOYMENT RELATIONSHIP (A Postclaim Root-Cause Analysis Can Reveal Valuable Lessons)

After being fired, Florence, a salesperson at one of my client's computer stores, filed a claim for sex discrimination and retaliation. Two years later, her case settled.

The amount of time and money this case consumed greatly displeased the CEO. As we left the plaintiff attorney's office where we finalized the settlement, he turned to me and said, "What do we need to do to make sure this doesn't happen again?"

We scheduled a meeting of his store managers where I played "coroner" and conducted an "autopsy" of Florence's lawsuit. We looked for three types of lessons:

1. How the claim could have been prevented altogether
2. How the claim might have been nipped in the bud instead of taking two years
3. What other insights into the company's processes and culture might be revealed

At the meeting, I pointed out the evidence that supported management's decision to fire Florence. This included low sales productivity, her often crude ways of speaking to employees and customers, and the discovery that she had a personal side business she'd failed to disclose in violation of company policy.

The evidence showed that problems with Florence's performance had existed for years, and that because of her offensive behavior, two employees had quit and several customers had switched to competitors. I said to the managers, "So firing this employee should have been a no-brainer, right?"

I then turned to the arrows in Florence's quiver. They included lack of progressive discipline and documentation of her performance and behavior problems.

Rather than confront Florence, the manager of her store, Bob, adopted an avoidance approach to dealing with her. A big reason was his fear of a sex-discrimination claim, which Florence alluded to in her own crass fashion: "Admit it Bob. You and the guys have a tough time working with someone who doesn't have a you-know-what between her legs."

Although Florence never brought a gender complaint to the attention of the human resources department, she claimed Bob had told her, "Talking to HR wouldn't be good for your future." Although he denied saying it, Bob's credibility was undermined by the fact that he'd never informed HR about Florence's complaints, performance problems, or offensive behavior.

Florence denied ever having received the policy regarding

employees having side businesses, and there was no convincing proof to show that she had.

Another important autopsy point: After Florence asserted her claim but before she'd hired an attorney, she offered to drop her claim in exchange for three months' severance pay. However, Bob had insisted that her claim was "worthless." As a result, there was no early scrutiny of the claim's strengths and weaknesses, and no negotiation.

When the claim finally did settle, the price plus accumulated attorneys' fees and costs added up to nearly $200,000, the equivalent of over two years' severance pay. And this price didn't include the numerous hours spent by company employees in legal proceedings.

Additional points covered in our session:

- ▸ The bigger the potential problem, the sooner it needs to be dealt with. To maximize the value of your human resources department, let it know early on when you're having an employee relations issue so it can help you develop and execute a game plan. Don't wait until the problem has become intolerable.
- ▸ Offensive speech such as Florence's should never be tolerated, even if the person using it claims to be a victim. Don't fall for "the best defense is a good offense."
- ▸ If a policy is important, the company should have a specific plan or practice to communicate it and to show that it has been communicated.

▸ When a claim is filed, an early and hard look should be taken. Otherwise, an opportunity for cost-effective settlement may be lost.

Following this session, management made several changes, including overhauling its training-and-development program and policy-implementation practices. Steps included creating guidelines for human resources-operations management interaction that would increase collaboration, communication-skills training in how to confront employee relations challenges, and use of the Same Day Summary documentation tool ("Texas Wes").

The results? The company reported improved productivity and accountability as well as a welcome long stretch where it remained claims free.

MORAL OF THE STORY

Conducting "autopsies" of employment claims is good for company business and bad for legal business.

If you've been involved in an employment claim that was resolved, you probably wanted nothing more than to put the experience behind you as quickly as possible. Most employers react this way, treating the resolved claim as a kidney stone that finally passed.

Yet this tendency should be resisted. As this story shows, there's an enormous upside to using that painful experience in the U.S. legal system as a catalyst for growth and positive change.

Every lawsuit or significant claim I dealt with contained valuable lessons for employers. These lessons aren't just confined to what employers can do to avoid future claims. They include insights into how employers can run their businesses better and get a better return on their human capital.

Workplace claims open a window into how your employees function in relation to the company's mission, values, and goals. Before the trail goes cold, identify takeaways for better practice. In addition, use the recently concluded claim to generate a sense of urgency and momentum for constructive change.

You paid dearly for your experience in the U.S. legal system. Why not get your money's worth?

THE RESCINDED RESIGNATION
(Telltale Signs You Employ a "Profile Plaintiff")

An immigrant from Eastern Europe worked in my client's information systems (IS) department as a systems analyst. Dmitri had a prickly personality. When problems arose, he quickly pointed his finger at others.

For example, when the IS director inquired about a customer complaint, Dmitri instantly became defensive: "It's not my fault! I did nothing wrong! Those people did not follow my instructions. They are stupid!"

Dmitri tended to keep to himself. When he did interact with other employees, it was typically to complain about deficient working conditions, management, customers, and coworkers.

Sometimes he complained about America. "You people are spoiled. You don't know what real work is." Another subject was his treatment as an immigrant. "They say America is a big melting pot. Some pot! I get mistreated here because I'm from another country and my English is maybe not 100 percent perfect. My wife gets mistreated too."

Without prompting, Dmitri brought up problems in his marriage. The reaction of his coworkers to hearing sensitive, personal life details from this otherwise cold and aloof man: "too much information."

Employees suspected that Dmitri had a drinking problem. He appeared visibly intoxicated at a company social function. In addition, one employee reported to his supervisor that he'd observed Dmitri behaving erratically at work and smelling of alcohol. However, no investigation was conducted.

Dmitri had enrolled in the company's educational support program through which he sought a computer science degree at a local college. After submitting the paperwork, Dmitri mentioned to the IS director that he intended to apply for a student loan even though his educational expenses would be fully covered by his employer. When asked why, Dmitri responded, "I'm going to use the money to pay off my car loan—better interest rate."

Although Dmitri's plan struck the manager as less than ethical and possibly even illegal, he figured this was a matter between Dmitri and the lender, not an issue for him or the company.

In the meantime, Dmitri was assigned a new supervisor, Pamela. Pamela felt management had been too lenient with Dmitri regarding his behavior. Things were going to change.

For the first time, Dmitri received counseling. Pamela told him: "You need to be less defensive. Stop blaming other people when things go wrong. Focus instead on improving your communication skills with employees and customers."

Although Pamela had not taken formal disciplinary action against him, Dmitri was incensed. His anger increased exponentially three months later when he read his annual performance review. Although Pamela rated his performance as acceptable overall, she noted deficits, including in his treatment of others.

Dmitri became so mad reading this criticism he got up from his desk and shouted, "I can't work with such idiots! I am done with this company!" With that, he gathered his personal belongings and stormed out the door.

Pamela was shocked when she first learned the news. "Oh my goodness!" she said to a coworker, "I was only trying to help him improve." That evening, she called him at home. By then, Dmitri had received an earful from his wife about his "impetuous and irresponsible decision that will hurt our children."

Pamela apologized for having upset him and explained, "I was only trying to help you be more successful." Although Dmitri still felt aggrieved and said so, he had calmed down considerably.

"Would you reconsider your decision to quit?" Pamela asked.

Dmitri responded with a lecture on the importance of "treating people from other countries with respect." He added that he would accept her offer.

Dmitri returned to work the next morning. All was not well, however. He displayed an empowered sense of victimhood. In his mind, he had humbled management. His problematic attitude got worse.

Eventually, Pamela initiated disciplinary proceedings against him, which sparked fresh outrage and complaints that he was being "discriminated against because I am a man from another country."

Dmitri's behavior continued to spiral downward and reached the point where management felt compelled to end his employment. Dmitri responded by filing claims of retaliation, harassment, and discrimination based on gender and national origin.

We ended up in court. Ultimately, we prevailed in showing that Dmitri's "maleness" and Eastern European origin had nothing to do with his discharge. However, the case went on much longer than my client expected because of documentation gaps and inconsistency in management's position that Dmitri was a long-time problem yet formal discipline had been administered only near the end of his employment.

By the time the case was dismissed, my client had paid a high price in time, money, and energy. Pamela had paid a high price in prolonged anxiety and stress, which impaired her ability to lead her department.

When the verdict came down in my client's favor, no high fives were exchanged. Instead, the client's reaction was a mixture of relief and exhaustion.

MORAL OF THE STORY

Beware of signs that you employ a Profile Plaintiff.

Long before the existence of the Transportation Security Administration, I wrote an article called "The Profile Plaintiff." In it, I made an analogy to airport security measures adopted in the 1970s following a spate of skyjackings by dissident groups. Airline passengers were starting to dread hearing messages over the plane's intercom like, "Ladies and gentlemen, you have boarded a flight from Chicago to New York—via Havana."

Airline security responded by creating profiles of passengers considered disproportionately likely to be skyjackers. Analyzing people who hijacked or attempted to hijack airplanes, they identified common characteristics to create the profile skyjacker. When a passenger met the profile, heightened security measures were implemented.

Based on having litigated numerous workplace disputes, I applied a similar methodology to employees disproportionately likely to sue their employers. From this, I came up with the Profile Plaintiff. Some characteristics may seem obvious, but some may not. Dmitri illustrated several profile plaintiff characteristics that management typically overlooks:

- **Has a chip-on-the-shoulder attitude.** Dmitri never admitted mistakes or acknowledged fault. Instead, he continually pointed the blame finger at others.

- **Complains of mistreatment due to protected class status.** Dmitri's maleness and Eastern European origin may not have been the most compelling of legally protected classifications. However, they were enough for him to assert victim status and use it as a basis for a retaliation claim.

- **Is alternatively aloof and volatile.** Dmitri had little interest in communicating with others, unless it was to vent over his latest sense of grievance.

- **Brings up problems from personal life.** Dmitri didn't have a monopoly on personal life challenges. The difference was Dmitri's urge to share them with coworkers even though they weren't his personal friends or confidants.

- **Has alcohol or substance-abuse issues**. Employees with drinking or substance-abuse problems, as

Dmitri may have had, disproportionately show up as plaintiffs.

► **Is dishonest**. When personally cheated, people see a red flag. Many, however, miss the connection between an employee's willingness to cheat others and, when it's in his or her interest, to cheat their company. Dmitri's obtaining a student loan on false pretenses may not have hurt the company, but it provided an important clue about his character, a clue the IS director missed.

► **Resigns in anger but is allowed to retract the resignation**. A telltale sign of future trouble is the employee who quits in a huff yet is allowed to return. Pamela's reaction to Dmitri's indignant "I'm out of here!" is not unusual. It's almost Pavlovian. The manager thinks, "His quitting will be a reflection on me," and tries talking the employee out of it. Yet in a calm, thoughtful moment, the manager would have acknowledged that the company would be better off without that employee. The result? More employment trouble and aggravation, and in some cases such as Dmitri's, an eventual messy termination followed by a lawsuit.

One profile characteristic standing alone doesn't signify a Profile Plaintiff. However, as with Dmitri, often many boxes are checked without management's lightbulb going on. As a result, it misses opportunities to manage the employee out of the workplace with relatively little or no trouble.

The solution is not to count boxes and fire somebody. Rather, it's to promptly and directly confront inappropriate employee behavior, promptly investigate evidence of misconduct, and let high-strung, high-maintenance employees accept the consequences of their rashness. Profile Plaintiffs can be managed out of a workplace with a surprising degree of efficacy. It takes a combination of early recognition and gumption to fix problems before they get worse.

THROWING STONES FROM A GLASS HOUSE
(Beware of Conditions That Problematic Employees Can Use Against You)

Fred was vice president of sales at a publicly traded medical-products company based in the southeast United States. As the company grew and expanded into new markets, Marissa, the company's CEO, increasingly had reservations about Fred's suitability for his position. Other members of the executive team had expressed concerns to Marissa about Fred's lack of vision, initiative, and leadership, and believed an upgrade would be needed for the company's long-term prosperity.

After mulling the matter over for a while, Marissa called Fred into her office. "Unfortunately, Fred," she said, "as we've grown, I don't believe you're the right person for the vice president job. I'm planning to conduct a national search for your successor. When the new vice president is hired, we can discuss whether there might still be a position for you here. However, if you want to start looking for another job in the meantime, that's fine with me."

Following this meeting, Fred wrote a letter to the chairman of the board of directors. In it, he alleged that Marissa had subjected him to unwelcome sexual conduct. Fred also alleged that Marissa had pressured him to make end-of-quarter sales to distributors that weren't viable and to allow the distributors to return the products for a full refund if they couldn't be sold. Fred claimed this was done to artificially inflate revenue and profitability numbers to shareholders.

Fred said in his letter, "I have resisted Marissa's sexual advances as well as her directives to violate the law. As a result, she's become hostile to me and is now threatening my job."

After Fred's letter, the board of directors hired an independent investigator to assess the validity of Fred's allegations. The investigator interviewed dozens of people and reviewed numerous documents and email correspondence.

Regarding Fred's sexual harassment claim, there was plenty of evidence that Marissa was a hugger. However, by all accounts, she hugged people of both genders indiscriminately and never hugged anyone in the "Velcro" manner Fred described. Moreover, there was no evidence that Fred ever complained about or expressed discomfort with her behavior. In fact, one employee recalled him complaining that Marissa failed to hug him after she returned from a business trip. Fred had asked the employee, "Do you think she's mad at me?"

Regarding Fred's allegation of improper business practices, there was evidence of questionable end-of-quarter sales followed by refunds in the next quarter. However, the evidence showed that Fred participated in this activity and didn't resist, much less blow the whistle until faced with termination for unrelated reasons.

The investigation concluded with a finding that Fred's complaints of sexual harassment and retaliation were not credible. Not long thereafter, the company fired him. Fred responded by filing claims with two government agencies.

Both agencies investigated Fred's claims and scrutinized the investigator's findings. Neither agency disputed the conclusion that Fred's treatment was due to legitimate business reasons, not unlawful retaliation.

End of story, right?

Wrong.

After the employment issues ended, a government agency continued investigating the company's end-of-quarter sales practices. Eventually, it brought criminal charges against Marissa. Fred testified for the prosecution. Following a lengthy trial, a jury convicted her on multiple felony counts. Prison time followed, and her previously distinguished career came to a ruinous end.

MORAL OF THE STORY

This story serves as a cautionary tale. Marissa was not an evil or corrupt person. However, as a CEO who had been lionized for her success, she felt increasing pressure to meet others' high expectations. This pressure tempted her down a slippery slope. Little by little, and without appreciating the consequences, she was picking up steam and heading toward the cliff. A self check-in might have saved her, but it didn't come until too late.

When leaders slip below fully ethical, principled behavior in their own conduct, it's difficult to hold employees accountable for their behavior. As Marissa learned the hard way, it can also be dangerous. Before looking out of your front window, observing and assessing others, it's useful to first take a look in the mirror. In your own behavior, have you set the example you wish to see in others?

BONUS MORAL OF THE STORY

In "An Employee Engagement Lesson Learned from a Volunteer Experience," I identified connecting on a personal level as one of the three pillars of engaged workplace relationships. There are limits, however. Although there was nothing sexual in Marissa's hugging, it did create vulnerability that a disgruntled employee could exploit. More importantly, during the investigation, some employees said they didn't like being hugged but were uncomfortable saying so to the company's CEO. Employees also said that Marissa's hugging practice gave rise to employee speculation. Since she was less apt to hug an out-of-favor employee, employees would speculate about who was or wasn't in her doghouse.

Save your hugs for family and friends. In the workplace, and especially when you occupy a position of power, your hugs can produce unintended and undesirable consequences. There are other ways to connect personally. This book describes a few. None require putting your arms around your employees.

THE FRUSTRATIONS OF MIDDLE MANAGEMENT
(Try an Alternative to Permission or Forgiveness Called "Per-Giveness")

When I became managing shareholder of a large law firm's Portland and Seattle offices, I had a new managerial experience. In the past, I had founded and managed a law firm and had served as president and chief administrative officer of a nonprofit corporation with a largely supportive, deferential board. In those circumstances, I had been a boss without really having a boss. This time, I was a boss with a boss, or even bosses.

This experience presented me with fresh challenges that middle managers know well. The situation reminded me of a former college athletics director. During his press conference to announce his resignation, he said, "Unfortunately, my responsibility greatly exceeded my authority."

I struggled with the fact that I had to manage these offices in the here and now but often needed authority that was thousands of miles away and preoccupied with other things. This translated into delay, indecision, and frustration, not only on my part but on those I managed who awaited direction from me.

Necessity being the mother of invention, I developed a way to combat this challenge. If you recall the Same Day Summary tool ("Texas Wes"), you could say this one was more of a Same Day Preview. I called it per-giveness: per(mission) + (for)giveness. First there would be an assessment of the decision I contemplated making. In which of these three categories did it belong?

1. **Permission:** Prior authorization from the boss is a necessity. The decision is too important. Without authorization, I don't go forward.
2. **Forgiveness:** As the saying goes, "Just do it." If things go wrong and my boss doesn't like what I did, I'll dust off a MIDAS Touch apology ("Apology Trilogy").
3. **Per-giveness:** I'll let the boss know (a) what I plan to do, (b) why I think it's a good idea, and (c) when I plan to do it. The boss will have an opportunity to weigh in, but it's not required.

For per-giveness, email came in handy. I'd write my boss a message, saying I plan to do X by Y date or time and add the reason. I wouldn't ask for his opinion. Instead, I'd conclude the message with something like, "Let me know if you have questions or wish to discuss this beforehand." If I didn't hear anything by Y, I implemented X. That simple.

The tool worked so well for me with my superiors that I taught it to a boss who had a boss: me. This was my office administrator. She managed the office staff and reported to me. Per-giveness became part of our delegation dialogue.

Certain decisions fell in the permission category. For example: "Jathan, I think the office needs to be remodeled. I have a bid of $47,000. May I go forward?" Others fell under forgiveness: "I authorized two hours of secretarial overtime yesterday evening." Still others fell in between, per-giveness: "Jathan, at my next staff meeting on Monday morning, I plan to announce a new protocol regarding vacation scheduling. It's intended to _____. Let me know if you have questions or wish to discuss this ahead of time."

My office administrator and I periodically assessed the types of decisions that belonged in each category and made adjustments. How did this help us? From my perspective as her boss, it promoted trust, confidence, and efficiency. I never had to worry, "What's she up to now?" Yet I wasn't bogged down or distracted having to make lots of decisions just to keep things running.

Also, I had a new option for decisions that fell in the gray area. When my office administrator gave notice of an impending action, I wasn't required either to endorse or reject her recommended action. If I was on the fence, I could read her per-giveness message and do nothing but let her act as she thinks appropriate.

From her standpoint, this three-category decision-making approach created a nice balance: management without micromanagement. Moreover, it eliminated the frustrating and even enervating experience of sending repeated requests to a boss who doesn't respond.

MORAL OF THE STORY

Per-giveness messages are simple. State the action you want to take, your reasons for doing so, and when you plan to act. Don't ask for your boss's opinion, only that the boss let you know if he or she has questions or wishes to discuss your planned action. If you hear nothing by the date and time specified, act.

As an employee, per-giveness will create for you a healthy balance between absentee management and micromanagement. You'll have more freedom to act with reassurance that you're on the same page with your boss. As a boss, per-giveness will keep you informed. You'll have an opportunity to weigh in but aren't required to do so. You can delegate responsibility without a hands-off-versus-micromanagement dichotomy. Also, if you're struggling with "Yes," "No," or "Maybe," you have another option: Quietly let your employee make the call. No more stewing in indecision while leaving your employee hanging.

Assuming you're persuaded to use the tool, I'll give you your first per-giveness message:

Hi Boss,

Please read the story about "per-giveness" in this Hard-Won Wisdom book that I've flagged for you. I plan to implement this tool starting next week. Let me know if you have questions or would like to discuss this concept ahead of time.

Best, You

IT'S THE EAR NOT THE ERR METHOD
(Put These Concepts and Tools to Work Sooner Rather Than Later)

I had been working with a group of restaurant managers on improving their leadership skills. After a two-month interval, I returned for a follow-up program.

In the previous workshop, I'd taught attendees the EAR method of listening. Readers of "If You Want Engagement, Lead by Listening" will recall that "E" stands for "explore" (open-ended questions), "A" is for "acknowledge" (confirming your understanding with the person you're listening to), and "R" is for "response" (which comes last.)

As I began the follow-up program, one of the managers

interrupted me. "Jathan," he said. "Before you get started, I have a question."

"Yes," I said.

With an edge in his voice, he said, "Remember when you were here two months ago and taught us that EAR listening thing?"

"Yes," I replied.

"Do you remember saying it's useful if we're dealing with employees who are upset?"

"Yes, I believe I said something along those lines."

His voice rising, the manager said, "Well I tried it last Friday, and it backfired!"

With a catch in my throat, I said, "What happened?"

"It was a busy Friday evening. One of our patrons, a big spender but somewhat of a pompous jerk, didn't get the table he wanted. He took it out on the hostess, a young gal who did a good job for us.

"I wasn't there at the time, but she came to me later and told me about the incident. I could see she was still upset so I thought that EAR thing might be useful. I asked her a bunch of questions about what happened: what she said, what he said, what the reservation book had in it, and so on. I then responded with what I thought was a good response.

"Instead, she got mad at me and said, 'You don't really care about the employee do you? You only care about the customer!'

"I got a little angry myself and told her she was totally wrong. Things got more heated. Soon she burst into tears and quit, right there on the spot, leaving me shorthanded on a crowded Friday night and now having to replace a good employee."

With dripping sarcasm, he added, "Thanks for your help, Jathan!"

Instinctively, my eyes searched for the exit. However, a woman who attended the prior session rescued me. She said to the manager, "I heard the Explore part and I heard your Response. However, I didn't hear the Acknowledge part where you confirmed your understanding about what had made her upset. Did you do that?"

The manager looked puzzled. "I don't remember," he said. "Maybe I skipped that part. Oops!"

I didn't have to run for the exit after all.

MORAL OF THE STORY

First of all, it's the EAR method not the ERR method, which is what this manager mistakenly applied. Instead of confirming his understanding with his employee before responding, he made an assumption. She took exception to it and made her own assumption about him (cares only about customers, not employees), and they were off to the races.

The manager made another and even more basic mistake. Consider the timing. He learned the EAR listening method two months before ever attempting to use it, even though the tool's designed to be used in daily communication. Instead, he held off until faced with an especially challenging situation with elevated emotions. Given the delay, is it any surprise he got it wrong?

I now tell my workshop attendees, "If you wait two months to try something you learn today and it doesn't work, don't complain to me. You violated the warranty!"

Studies show that we start forgetting almost as quickly as we learn. This means new skills should be practiced as soon as possible, preferably within 72 hours. Otherwise, the risk of omitting or misapplying a crucial detail goes up dramatically. It's a use-it-(soon)-or-lose-it proposition.

Although you can return to the book for a refresher, I encourage you to apply the 72-hour rule. Pick something you learned from the book that resonates with you. Perhaps it's the EAR method, the Triple Two, or Per-giveness. Perhaps it's the What/Why Ratio, the Period/Question-Mark Ratio, or the Same Day Summary. Perhaps it's the Star Profile, MIDAS Touch apology, or Monks Technique. Whatever it is, put it to work now.

Motivation without action doesn't last. Neither does action without results. However, when you combine all three, you can achieve sustained meaningful change.

Here are questions to get you going. I encourage you to answer them in writing.

▶ Having read this book, what concepts or tools strike you as worthy of using?

- ► What specific steps will you commit to take, and by when?
- ► What results do you expect to see?

That writing will serve as your first roadmap in moving from theory to practice to results. Have a great journey!

INDEX